Young Vic THEATRE UNCUT

A Young Vic and Theatre Uncut co-production

C000162675

Chasing Hares

by Sonali Bhattacharyya

Winner of the Theatre Uncut Political Playwriting Award 2021

CHASING HARES

By Sonali Bhattacharyya

Chasing Hares had its world premiere at the Young Vic on 16 July 2022.

CAST (in alphabetical order)

Chellam	Ayesha Dharker
Kajol	Zainab Hasan
Devesh	Scott Karim
Amba	Saroja-Lily Ratnavel
Prab	Irfan Shamji

CREATIVE TEAM

Director	Milli Bhatia
Designer	Moi Tran
Lighting Designer	Jai Morjaria
Video Designer	Akhila Krishnan
Sound Designer	Donato Wharton
Composer	Sarathy Korwar
Movement Director	Chi-San Howard
Voice and Dialect Coach	Gurkiran Kaur
Fight Director	Bret Yount
Casting Director	Polly Jerrold
Assistant Director	Nikhil Vyas
Assistant Director	Ashen Gupta
Trainee Assistant Director	Tia Ali
R & D Lyric Consultant	Jammz
R & D Dramaturg	Guy Jones
Producer	Bella Rodrigues

Special thanks to: Piali Ray, Guy Jones, Jammz, Paul Miller, Indhu Rubasingham, Anna Himali-Howard, Adrian Kawaley-Lathan and the Bertha Foundation Artivism team, The Peggy Ramsay Foundation, Film4 and everyone at the Channel 4 Playwrights' Scheme, National Theatre, Unicorn Theatre

Chasing Hares is generously supported by Patrick Handley & Louis Deshpande.

Young Vic

About the Young Vic

For fifty years, the Young Vic has produced new plays, classics, musicals, adaptations of books, short films, digital projects and game-changing forms of theatre, attracting large audiences from many different backgrounds.

They forge deep connections in their neighbourhood through their ambitious Taking Part programme, where they engage with over 15,000 people every year via a wide range of projects, helping their community to develop their creative skills, build meaningful relationships, and tell compelling stories about the world we live in. The Young Vic give 10% of their tickets free to those who experience the biggest barriers accessing the arts, irrespective of box office demand, and they are committed to keeping their ticket prices low.

The Young Vic's Creators Program is our space for multi- and anti-disciplinary artists, and is the only scheme of its kind. Launched in 2001 and formerly known as the Directors Program, we offer artists and producers a unique opportunity to develop their craft through skills workshops, peer-led projects, and paid work opportunities that range from trainee and assistant director roles to a two year residency through the Genesis Fellow/Associate Director position. The Genesis Network provides an online community to over 2,000 artists and producers. Each year, the recipient of the Genesis Future Directors Award directs a show in The Clare Theatre with full support from the Young Vic's creative, administrative and production teams, enabling us to support and nurture an early career director as part of our season of work.

For many years, the Young Vic has been synonymous with inclusivity, accessibility and creativity. They catalyse debate and channel their work into the digital world, to reach new audiences and continue conversations outside of their four walls. The Young Vic foster emerging talent and collaborate with some of the world's finest directors, performers and creatives; creating award-winning productions which engage with the world we live in.

Artistic Director   Kwame Kwei-Armah
Executive Director   Lucy Davies

youngvic.org

Public Support

 ARTS COUNCIL ENGLAND   HM Government   HERE FOR CULTURE   **Lambeth**   Southwark Council

Season Support

 BANK OF AMERICA   Garfield Weston FOUNDATION

The Young Vic's 2022 season is also supported by the Genesis Foundation and IHS Markit.

We gratefully acknowledge Ian Burford and Alec Cannell for generously supporting the Young Vic's mission.

THEATRE
UNCUT

Theatre Uncut make bold, progressive, political theatre for everyone, everywhere. They work with the world's leading and emerging playwrights. Theatre Uncut plays are tools for change and have been performed in 26 countries across 4 continents and viewed by over 200,000 people online. The Theatre Uncut Political Playwriting Award was launched to discover the next generation of political voices. The award was made possible by the Arts Council England's Emergency Response Fund, Creative Recovery Fund and in partnership with the Young Vic, Traverse Theatre, Sherman Theatre, Lyric Theatre Belfast, Independent Talent and Nick Hern Books.

Artistic Director   Emma Callander
Founder   Hannah Price

www.theatreuncut.com

CHASING HARES

Sonali Bhattacharyya

For Gargi, for Avijit,
for all the dreamers, all the organisers,
all the people making good trouble to win a better world.
And for Leela and Akash, always.

'If it was a matter of hunting a deer, everyone well realised that he must remain faithful to his post; but if a hare happened to pass within reach of one of them, we cannot doubt that he would have gone off in pursuit of it without scruple...'

Jean-Jacques Rousseau, A Discourse on Inequality

Characters

AMBA, *late twenties*
PRAB, *early thirties*
KAJOL, *early thirties*
DEVESH, *late twenties*
CHELLAM, *thirties*

Plus:

AUDIENCE MEMBER 1
AUDIENCE MEMBER 2
EATRIGHTNOW RIDER 1
EATRIGHTNOW RIDER 2
EATRIGHTNOW RIDER 3
JOURNALIST

*The actors playing Kajol, Devesh and Chellam double as
EatRightNow Riders 1, 2 and 3, the actor playing adult Amba
doubles as Audience Member and Journalist, and the actor
playing Kajol doubles as Audience Member 2.*

All actors should speak in their own accents.

A forward slash (/) indicates an interruption.

Words in [square brackets] are unspoken.

*This text went to press before the end of rehearsals and so may
differ slightly from the play as performed.*

Prologue

Late night, tonight. AMBA, late twenties, sits on a bench in the 'Login Zone' in Leicester town centre, a sleeping baby lying on her chest. She wears her EatRightNow uniform – a Deliveroo-type takeaway food courier. Her bike is propped up against a wall beside her.

AMBA (*to the baby*). Shh, shh, babs. Chandi lives next to this river, with Arun, her best friend, the monkey. And their neighbours are their friends. From the rabbits, and the weasels, to the beavers and the magpies, from the lizards and the frogs to the snakes and the squirrels. And the rabbits always bring back enough carrots and radishes for everyone to share. The beavers always make sure there are enough fish in the water for everyone to eat. The birds make sure the roof of everyone's home is strong and sturdy against the rain. The lizards make sure the mosquitoes don't swarm around their homes. But now there are these two ogre brothers, Sengupta and Chandok Sri, and they're fighting it out over who's the richest and they're working the land too hard and it's become so dry, and Chandi and the animals have to travel twice as far and work twice as hard to find half as much to eat. And Chandi wonders why these brothers have so much power over them? Why she and her friends are so scared of a couple of hairy ogres? If the fear beating in their hearts is the point. To stop them from looking up. Stop them from seeing the stars, let alone reaching for them... And she asks herself what could make them find the courage to take them on...?

She trails off, kisses her baby on the head and rubs his back, checking her watch, watching and waiting with nervous anticipation. The baby starts to cry.

Oh no, no no no. It's okay. It's okay, babs. Don't cry. Shh shh.

The baby cries harder. AMBA stands up and starts to pace and rock the baby.

(*To the baby.*) If my love were money
Would it be worth much more?
What price must I pay
To fight my own cause?

But I'm crying for nothing
I'm crying for nothing
Cos my loving heart is worth nothing at all.

*She sniffs his bottom. Loosens his snowsuit. Unzips her
hoodie halfway and puts him to her breast. He just cries
harder.*

What is it? What's up? It's okay, it's okay. (*She roots around
in her rucksack and produces a toy.*) Look, look, look.

He continues to cry.

What was Chandi doing? Hey? Hey, lovely? What does
Chandi do, when everything seems lost and broken? Does she
give up? No. She knows when Chandi calls, her friends
answer. So she puts two fingers in her mouth, and she whistles.

PRAB *enters, nonchalant, and sits down beside them. Kisses
the baby on the forehead. Maybe rolls a cigarette, or drinks
from a plastic bottle of water. The baby quietens for a
moment.*

And she… whistles. And the ogres look up, and before they
can say anything, a great flock of eagles have lifted them up,
up, up into the air. Chandi waves and laughs as they fly them
away from the forest, so far they'll never be able to bother
her or her friends again.

PRAB. That's not how it goes, Amba.

AMBA. We do the child-friendly version.

PRAB. Mine has talking animals in it. Children *love* talking
animals.

AMBA. So does mine. Just not getting their eyes gouged out by
ogres and shit.

PRAB. Sorry I'm late.

AMBA. You're not, Dad.

PRAB. Bit late for the little one though, isn't it?

AMBA. He sleeps where he wants, shits where he wants. Don't have to worry about him.

PRAB. He looks just like me.

AMBA. No he doesn't.

PRAB. Come on – look at that chin.

AMBA. He takes after Kav's side.

PRAB. Handsome little bastard. Wouldn't you rather be at home with him, watching TV, cuddling on the sofa?

AMBA. Kav was offered a night shift last minute. Can't turn anything down right now. He had to shoot over and leave babs with me.

PRAB. Can't your mum take him?

AMBA. She's working too.

PRAB. It's not right, you back at work so soon.

AMBA. Been so quiet today I might as well have stopped in.

She passes him her phone. He inspects it closely.

We're in Login Zone Three. See? Still nothing.

PRAB. Sounds like Khub Bhalo.

AMBA. It's a warm night – people have probably stayed out after work, got something to eat at the pub. It's not the same thing.

PRAB. I turned up at the factory gates one morning and they said 'no orders'. Come back tomorrow. Tomorrow turned into next week. Next week turned into next month. Next month turned into next year…

AMBA. Yeah yeah yeah. Way to keep my spirits up, Dad.

AMBA *stands up and starts rocking and swaying the baby.*

PRAB. Don't you get time off, with the baby? Your company should cover that.

AMBA. EatRightNow's an app, not a company. And I'm self-employed.

PRAB. *Great* Britain. They're so *civilised* here.

AMBA. They've got EatRightNow Kolkata now, you know? I saw it online.

PRAB. You look tired.

AMBA. Don't look so hot yourself.

PRAB. Why don't you call it a night, chotto?

AMBA. I'm meeting someone.

PRAB. Who?

AMBA. Some... friends. Colleagues.

AMBA *tries to breastfeed the baby again and this time he settles. She stands, rocking him, feeding him, maybe humming or quietly singing.*

One of them, Grant, he got his bike nicked this morning. We're getting together to see what people can chip in.

PRAB. That's nice.

AMBA. Don't have anything spare this month, but I brought along this extra front light...

She shows him the bike light, maybe she turns it on.

PRAB. He'll appreciate that.

AMBA. Don't know. Hope so.

PRAB. Have you all done this before...?

AMBA. Sort of. Ruby got assaulted by this customer one time? He tried to shove his hand down her top and she pushed him over in the communal hallway. Bastard made a complaint against *her*, and EatRightNow deactivated her account. She took it all the way to the top, but they still said she'd have to start the recruitment process again. And she was like 'Rent's due now.' So we got together and covered her for a few weeks until she was back on the app.

PRAB. Must have taken a lot of planning.

AMBA. Not really.

PRAB. Pretty short-termist though.

AMBA. Well that's what it's like for us. Day to day.

PRAB. Does it have to be?

AMBA.…I don't know.

PRAB. You're not the sort of person to suck it up.

AMBA. Everyone's that sort of person. When you've got three mouths to feed.

Beat.

You know… I heard riders in Newcastle get six quid an hour *and* two quid per drop.

PRAB. That's not what you get?

AMBA. I've only ever got a piece rate. Imagine if I was getting six quid an hour for waiting around in Login Zone Three?

PRAB. This shift would have been worth your while?

AMBA. Would have been worth *something*.

Beat.

And I keep thinking, how come they can do that for riders up there? What's so different about Newcastle?

PRAB. Never been there.

AMBA. You know what I mean.

PRAB. Same rent to pay?

AMBA. Same mouths to feed.

PRAB. Sounds like you have an *idea*, chotto…

AMBA. Nope.

PRAB. Sounds like you have a *plan*.

AMBA. Anyone can have a plan.

PRAB. And sometimes when you say it out loud, you realise you all have the same idea.

AMBA. No way. There's over a hundred people on the RiderChat.

PRAB. So?

AMBA. So what if they all turn up?

PRAB. You can tell them about Newcastle.

AMBA. And then what?

PRAB. You can ask them what's so different up there?

AMBA. You don't know these people, they can smell bullshit a mile off.

PRAB. You don't smell of bullshit.

AMBA. You have to say that, you're my dad.

PRAB. When Chandi whistles...

AMBA. I'm not a kid any more.

PRAB. You know you used to catch every little cold and sniffle going when you were a baby? You'd get so bunged up we couldn't put you down to sleep. We had to take it in turns, sitting up in bed, resting you on our chests. Your mum had a special technique, involved four bolster pillows and a shawl. She could always fall asleep with you. But I was too scared. I'd just stay up. We got this plug-in eucalyptus thing that seemed to help a bit. It was a night light too. Worked out it was perfect for throwing shadow puppets. I started to make up stories – partly to keep myself awake. But in the dark and the quiet, with you in my arms, it felt like anything was possible.

AMBA. ...Doesn't feel like that now though.

PRAB. Are you sure, chotto?

PART ONE

Scene One

The early 2000s, inner-city Kolkata. PRAB *is in the room where he lives with his wife* KAJOL *and baby daughter, Amba, in the apartment they share with* KAJOL*'s parents, brother and sister-in-law.* PRAB *sits on the bed holding a swaddled baby Amba in his arms. He's reclining, telling her a bedtime story, at one with the past, the present and the future, doing what he does best – making it up as he goes along. He casts the occasional hand shadow puppet on the wall, using the dim glow of a cheap plug-in Micky Mouse night light.*

PRAB. Chandi met Sengupta the ogre at the mouth of the river, as agreed. (*Enthusiastic ogre impression.*) 'O Chandi, some of your precious villagers spoke of your bravery, shortly before I ate them. But they didn't mention your phenomenal *stupidity.*' (*Fearsome ogre laugh.*) 'Now you will be reunited with them as you're digested together.' He lunges at her with his terrific claws. They're five times the size of the falcons' who hunt in the forest next to her village. But what do you think she does, Amba? Does she run? Does she cry? This is Chandi we're talking about. However big the ogre, however scary, she knows she's two steps ahead, and that makes her brave. And when Chandi calls, her friends answer. So she puts her fingers in her mouth and whistles. The loudest, most piercing whistle *ever.* Sengupta is so surprised he stops in his tracks and puts his warty hands over his ears. But then he starts to laugh. 'This is your final living act on earth? How pathetic.' Chandi responds with two words: 'Look up.' First he hears the beating of their wings. So many of them it sounds like drums. Then they come into view. Hundreds, no *thousands.* No. *Millions* of falcons. Falcons from every part of the forest, falcons from forests in the neighbouring kingdom, and the one beyond that, and the one *beyond that.*

Razor beaks wide open, waiting to taste this meaty ogre flesh they have heard so much about. The sky darkens as they descend. 'Arrrrgggggggghhhhhhh, my eyes...!' Chandi turns away. She will not gloat over her victory. She's too good for that.

KAJOL *enters, checks her sari in the mirror.*

KAJOL. A million falcons? You really think that's appropriate?

PRAB. Ah, you were eavesdropping.

KAJOL. No.

PRAB. You were *gripped*, you couldn't tear yourself away.

KAJOL. Time to go.

PRAB. I haven't finished.

KAJOL. Hate to tell you, Prab. I don't think she appreciates every single plot point.

PRAB *(to Amba)*. Don't listen to her.

KAJOL. Ore baba, she's already asleep. Come on, rush hour in Kolkata. You're going to make us miss the start.

PRAB *reluctantly kisses Amba on the forehead and bundles her into her Moses basket.*

PRAB. We're just going to talk about her all evening anyway.

KAJOL. *Chellam Dey*'s performing tonight.

PRAB *(melodramatic)*. 'The Story of Draupadi.' Yawn.

KAJOL. I heard they fired one of the troupe last week.

PRAB. What?

KAJOL. Apparently he grabbed her breast in the sari scene. Right there onstage. What a bastard. Doing that to *Chellam Dey*. He's not fit to kiss her sandals.

PRAB. Was anyone even there to see it? No one's interested in jatra any more.

KAJOL. *I* am.

PRAB. Yeah… But, you know…

KAJOL. No I don't know.

PRAB. Not everyone's as… romantic as you.

KAJOL. You can say that again. (*Of her sari.*) So glad I made an effort.

PRAB. …Shit is that… new?

KAJOL. What do you care?

PRAB. Was it… expensive?

KAJOL. Borrowed it off my cousin – don't worry.

PRAB. …Ravishing. What are you doing to me? Wow… She won't mind if it gets creased…?

KAJOL. I should be so lucky.

PRAB *does his ogre impression again, lunging at* KAJOL, *ending up in a flirtatious embrace.*

Shh. You'll wake her up.

PRAB. I can stay back if you like? Make sure she's settled.

KAJOL. Stop talking, right now. You'd rather spend time with Amba and her imaginary friends?

PRAB. I have to be at the factory at five a.m.

KAJOL. You can afford to miss one early shift of waiting around for nothing.

PRAB. Heard a rumour they're reopening. Don't want to skip the one morning it finally happens.

KAJOL. That rumour goes round every week.

PRAB. Heard there were some big shots from America in town. Or Australia. Maybe there's a Western order incoming.

KAJOL. Oh, they want Indian labour again?

PRAB. Major strike action in Vietnam. Their supply chain is fucked. They need a hero factory. Khub Bhalo could be up and running again just like that – (*Clicks his fingers.*)

KAJOL. Or they're just here to pick over the carcass.

PRAB. Well, then we can all finally commit to *doing* something.

KAJOL. Doing what?

PRAB. We're all on our best behaviour in case Khub Bhalo reopens. If the factory shuts down for good, we have nothing to lose. Can finally let them have it.

KAJOL. '*We*'?

PRAB. Every morning the talk is getting more militant. People are starting to ask why the Nags are sitting pretty while we're all struggling.

KAJOL. And you're keeping your mouth shut, aren't you? Because you're a dad now. They're going to have their pick of workers when they start up again – Nag isn't going to risk hiring troublemakers.

PRAB. Who's being optimistic now?

KAJOL. Everyone I know from Khub Bhalo is going to the jatra. If there is a big Western order incoming, someone will know about it.

PRAB (*of Amba*). What if she wakes up, though?

KAJOL. Ma knows how to settle her.

PRAB. She sleeps more soundly with a Chandi story though.

KAJOL. You might as well be reading her the cricket scores.

PRAB. Chandi is an important part of Amba's life. Hasn't she been hearing about her since she was in the *womb*?

KAJOL. I know, I thought you'd grow out of it.

PRAB. Chandi is resourceful, intelligent, principled. She's the role model every girl needs.

KAJOL. I'm not good enough for her, then?

PRAB.... Yes. Of course she is lucky to have you...

KAJOL *is genuinely interested to hear how he'll dig his way out of this one.*

But in Chandi's world, she doesn't have to pretend to be less resourceful, intelligent and principled than she is to avoid scaring the shit out of rich and powerful bastards.

KAJOL. Sounds nice.

PRAB. It is.

He sneaks a kiss. She softens.

KAJOL. Okay. We can argue later. Ma can only sit with her for a couple of hours.

She grabs him. They exit.

Scene Two

A traditional Bengali folk theatre (jatra) troupe perform in the round, in a pop-up open-air theatre. This is populist folk theatre. Opening classical Indian music plays offstage – maybe the traditional clarinet plus harmonium, or a contemporary version of this. DEVESH, *late twenties, enters, high energy, as Vivek (Conscience).*

DEVESH (*as Vivek*). Hello, Kolkata, how are you doing tonight? Hello to all the ladies, gentlemen, babies, bastards, grifters, loafers, scroungers, big dicks, small tits, and everyone in-between. Welcome, welcome, welcome. How are you doing?

He encourages the audience to respond.

Come on, I said, how are you *doing*?

Beat.

Really? We have the one, the only *Chellam Dey* backstage, right now, but honestly I'm wondering if we should even bring her on. I'm wondering if you're a worthy audience for her.

He looks backstage, shrugs melodramatically.

Are you a worthy audience for Chellam Dey – *the* Chellam Dey? Are you? Let me hear you if you are. Che-llam Dey, Che-llam Dey, Che-llam Dey, Che-llam Dey.

He continues chanting Chellam's name, encouraging the audience to call out and clap along.

Louder! At the back – let me hear you. Up there – let me hear you. You, over there. You can do better than that. Come on. I've got my eye on you. So, here we are, in the court of the richest, wisest, most powerful Lord Duryodhana. His sworn enemy, Lord Yudhistira, has gambled away all his riches, all his land, his brothers, his life and even his wife, Draupadi, in a high-stakes shooting match. And now Draupadi prepares to enter Duryodhana's court for the first time.

CHELLAM, *thirties, enters as Draupadi. She oozes glamour and sophistication despite her surroundings.*

It's a fact of life, the debt must be paid. As sure as the world spins on its axis, or the sun blazes down upon us. As certain as the wheels of time. Yudhistira ran out of luck but he kept his honour. We all know, there is no greater shame than a debt unpaid.

CHELLAM. Here I am, Draupadi. A caged bird trying to find her voice. And look, marble floors under my feet, silk tapestries on the walls of my cage. Peacocks strutting past. But none of this can mask the stench of injustice. I have been bartered like a bag of rice. How can I, Draupadi, ever accept this?

CHELLAM *performs a woeful song as Draupadi.*

(*Singing.*) I gave him my heart,
To be tossed aside,
This is how he repays me,
His pure-hearted bride.

But I'm crying for nothing
I'm crying for nothing
Cos my loving heart is worth nothing at all
Cos my loving heart is worth nothing at all.

If my love were money
Would it be worth much more?
What price must I pay
To fight my own cause?

But I'm crying for nothing
I'm crying for nothing
Cos my loving heart is worth nothing at all
Cos my loving heart is worth nothing at all.

(*Speaking*.) Duryodhana! He approaches!

Offstage, the sound of lightning and thunder, then classical Indian music begins to play.

Scene Three

Two hours later. PRAB *and* KAJOL *get up from their seats as the jatra ends, the same offstage music playing that marked the introduction.*

PRAB. Wow.

KAJOL. Oh, so you're a fan now, are you?

PRAB. She was good. She was really good. Did you feel that crackle in the air when she started singing? A woman over there started crying.

KAJOL. Told you she was worth seeing.

PRAB. Not like that Hritik Roshan wannabe, preening away. *She* was really connecting with people.

KAJOL. Prab, that wannabe is *Nag*'s son. Inheritor of the Khub Bhalo empire.

PRAB. No way.

KAJOL. Thought you knew that?

PRAB. Yeah but I thought it was just rumours. What's he doing wasting his time in the jatra...? Should be doing a business degree in Vancouver or somewhere.

KAJOL. Looks like Nag's throwing cash at vanity projects while the factory's on lockdown. Bastard.

PRAB *motions for her to keep her voice down.*

PRAB. Let's go backstage. Say hello.

KAJOL. What?

PRAB. Don't you want to meet the 'great Chellam Dey'?

KAJOL. No. What would I say to her?

PRAB. 'I've been pestering my husband to see this for weeks'...? Then maybe if the factory ever opens again... *when* it opens again, Nag Junior will tell his dad. 'Oh, that Prab's a cultured and intelligent fellow, he's the man we need on the shop floor.'

KAJOL. What if he's heard about you? What if he recognises your name?

PRAB. Ore baba, it was the Student Federation not the Bolshevik army.

KAJOL. Same difference to them.

PRAB. He's the new generation, isn't he? He loves jatra, the arts... Maybe he's not like his dad. This could be my chance to... start a clean slate.

KAJOL. You'll get excited and shoot your mouth off. Say something off-colour, give them a full review of the show they didn't ask for. Then it'll be 'That Prab's annoying and opinionated, I never want to see him again as I long as I live.'

PRAB. Am I an idiot?

KAJOL. Oh, you won't *plan* to, but the moment will overtake you and all of a sudden you'll find yourself having some sort of heated debate...

PRAB. I am *not* here for a heated debate. I will be polite. I will be... *complimentary*.

KAJOL. Praise upon praise. Especially about him. And... talk about the song at the end. Be specific, be positive.

PRAB. What's this, a lesson in arse-licking?

KAJOL. This is how people get ahead. Doesn't matter how hard you work, how fast you are. What really matters is how effectively you can lick Nag's backside.

They exit.

Scene Four

CHELLAM *is removing her make-up in the bare, makeshift dressing room.*

CHELLAM. Did you see those guys in the front row leering at me?

DEVESH. The front row? They were decrepit.

CHELLAM. They can still see, can't they? And hear. Everyone's talking about Adhil and his busy hands. My reputation's mud in this city.

DEVESH. Oh save the melodrama. You're not on the clock any more.

CHELLAM. And we're still wheeling out his half-baked plays. It's like I have that pervert looking over my shoulder every damn day.

DEVESH. I had him taken care of.

CHELLAM. If we don't get some new material soon, I'm done.

DEVESH. You changed half his lines.

CHELLAM. But I'm an actor, not a writer.

DEVESH. Any writer with ambition has their sights on Mumbai.

CHELLAM. No one wants to work with us because all we ever do are these tedious adaptations of the fucking *Mahabharata*.

DEVESH. The *Mahabharata*'s beneath you now?

CHELLAM. It's two thousand years old – time we changed the record.

DEVESH. One-point-two billion Hindus can't be wrong.

CHELLAM. Not sure if you've noticed, but they're not buying tickets.

DEVESH. Not sure if you've noticed, but you're not Sushmita Sen. Be realistic.

A knock at the door.

CHELLAM. Who is it?

DEVESH. I ordered champagne.

CHELLAM *opens the door.* PRAB *and* KAJOL *enter.*

PRAB. Hello. Sorry to disturb you.

DEVESH. Fucking security guards – chewing paan and playing cards as usual.

PRAB. They let us in because they recognised me. I used to work at Khub Bhalo. We just wanted to say how *much* we enjoyed the show.

CHELLAM. That's good to hear. The front row were total pigs tonight.

PRAB. But you were really *professional*.

KAJOL *glares at him.*

DEVESH (*to* CHELLAM). There you go – that's one to put on the poster.

KAJOL. He means you were great, he means you were *fantastic*. You have such star quality. It was impossible to take our eyes off you.

CHELLAM. Thank you.

KAJOL. And your voice is *excellent*.

PRAB. *Really* excellent.

DEVESH (*to* CHELLAM). Struggled with the high notes today, didn't you?

CHELLAM. No, not really.

DEVESH. I heard a *bit* of a crack. (*Sings a high note badly.*)

CHELLAM. Ignore him – thinks he's a comedian.

PRAB *can't help but laugh.* DEVESH *glares at him.*

PRAB (*to* DEVESH). Must be why you have such fantastic timing.

DEVESH. Oh...?

PRAB. You also brought real... *tension* to the scene.

CHELLAM. Did the show connect with you, Prab? The characters, I mean? Did their... problems chime with your own, in any way?

PRAB (*to* CHELLAM). You certainly had the audience in the palm of your hand. Even with a story that's so... familiar to them...

DEVESH. Baba appreciates the classics. He says there's a reason they've lasted so long – offered us wisdom from the Mughals, to the British, to fucking iPods and coffee shops.

PRAB. It's incredible he finds time to run a successful business and be so involved in the arts.

DEVESH. Are you taking the piss?

PRAB....No. Sir...

DEVESH. Factory's been locked up for months.

PRAB. I know, but that's surely a... shrewd business decision. He must have to make a lot of tough choices to run that place.

CHELLAM (*to* PRAB). I want to know what *you* thought?

DEVESH. He just said.

CHELLAM. No he didn't. This is the problem. You have no interest in what our audience thinks.

KAJOL. Prab has a degree in Bengali Literature.

PRAB *nudges* KAJOL *to shut up.*

It's how he first caught my eye, actually. I saw him at the coffee house telling some girl an idea he had for a novel / and...

PRAB. Just a book of short stories. I was young –

KAJOL.... it was clear he was boring her senseless, but I liked the sound of it.

CHELLAM. That's actually quite romantic.

PRAB (*to* KAJOL). You never told me that.

KAJOL. You never asked.

CHELLAM (*to* DEVESH). There you go. You underestimate people.

DEVESH. Wow, we have Rabindranath Tagore himself in tonight.

All eyes on PRAB. *Awkward beat.*

PRAB. Well, it was really... scary, when, um, Draupadi was faced with Duryodhana / in his court.

CHELLAM. It meant something to you? A couple of high-caste bastards fighting over some poor woman? And she's only saved because she's already on her knees to Krishna.

PRAB. I... well...

CHELLAM. That's something you've experienced in your own life? Divine intervention?

PRAB. No. But there's still time...

CHELLAM (*to* DEVESH). I like him.

DEVESH. He's just some factory monkey trying to impress you. (*To* PRAB.) What are you after? (*Of* CHELLAM.) Something to remember later when your wife's asleep?

KAJOL. Er, excuse me, but that is not / acceptable...

PRAB (*to* DEVESH). Can I ask who writes your jatras, sir?

DEVESH. Guy called Adhil.

CHELLAM. No longer with us.

PRAB. He's dead?

CHELLAM. Unfortunately not.

DEVESH. Close though.

PRAB. Okay, forgive my... candour.

CHELLAM. Go for it.

PRAB. I think, in my opinion, that maybe with a story as familiar as this one, you can afford to take some risks. Just a... few...

CHELLAM. Tell a story that actually means something to the ordinary fucker in the crowd?

DEVESH (*to* CHELLAM). What do you know about ordinary?

CHELLAM. I know our audience. Fishmongers, auto wallahs, machine operators...

DEVESH. *I* know our audience. Half of them are outside the gates at Khub Bhalo every morning.

CHELLAM (*to* PRAB). What's your idea?

PRAB....My idea...?

CHELLAM. *Yes*. Do you still write? We're interested in exploring a new direction.

PRAB. Well…

DEVESH. You've got us fired up with your insightful fuckery, don't leave us with blue balls.

PRAB. Actually, I am working on something at the moment.

CHELLAM. Okay…?

PRAB. Something based on the greatest untold Indian myth of all time. The one scholars have edited out of the *Mahabharata* over the centuries…

KAJOL *shoots him a querying look*.

DEVESH. Vikarna?

PRAB. No.

DEVESH. Ahilawati?

PRAB. No.

CHELLAM. Her son…? The story of Barbarik?

PRAB. No, not Barbarik… His… daughter.

DEVESH. I've never heard of him having a child.

PRAB. No one has.

CHELLAM. What's his name?

PRAB. *Her* name is…

KAJOL *discreetly shakes her head at him*.

Chandi. And her story is full of danger and cunning and sacrifice and… the highest stakes of all.

CHELLAM. Why? What does she do?

PRAB *has to think on his feet*.

PRAB.…After Barbarik's ultimate self-sacrifice, baby Chandi is secreted to safety, to escape the wrath of the Kauravas, who blame their defeat on her father. As she grows up, she unwittingly continues his legacy, protecting the weak and the vulnerable wherever she goes.

Unimpressed beat.

DEVESH. How does she do that? Nag them to death? No wait, maybe she sharpens her high heels and uses them to… (*Stabbing motion.*)

CHELLAM (*to* DEVESH). Fuck you.

PRAB. Chandi is small, but she knows this makes her strong.

DEVESH. Small but strong…? Like a… goat?

PRAB. Like a *diamond*.

DEVESH. Hmm.

PRAB. Her enemies underestimate her. And she is cunning, and wise beyond her years, and speaks in such a way that people rally to her cause.

DEVESH. Sounds like Gandhi in a skirt. I mean. A real skirt.

CHELLAM. Rally to what cause?

PRAB. Um, well, at its heart this is a story of… emancipation…

CHELLAM. Led by her?

PRAB. Yes. She inspires people.

CHELLAM. Like a muse?

PRAB. No, no. Like a leader. A bold and intelligent leader.

CHELLAM.…Interesting.

DEVESH. Might get more women in. (*To* PRAB.) Are you in the union?

KAJOL. / No no.

PRAB. / No, definitely not.

DEVESH. Communist?

KAJOL. / Ore *baba* – no way!

PRAB. No, *sir*. I'm not political. Not at all. Never have been. I'm a company man. I loved it at Khub Bhalo. Can't wait to return.

DEVESH. Alright, alright, take it down a bit. It's okay to be pissed off. I couldn't give a shit what you do in your spare time, but Baba will. Can you write us some scenes?

PRAB. Can... I... write some... [scenes]?

DEVESH. Are you deaf or something? Can. You. Write. Us. Some. Scenes?

KAJOL. He would be *honoured*.

PRAB. Of course I can.

CHELLAM. Excellent. Can't wait.

DEVESH. You've got two weeks. (*Slapping* PRAB *on the back*.) It's called an opportunity, my friend. You look like I told you I'm fucking your sister.

PRAB *tries his best to laugh*.

Do you have a sister?

PRAB. No.

DEVESH. Lighten up, lighten up. We rehearse in the back room of the factory. Bring them over when you're done and if they're any good, we'll take you on.

CHELLAM *gives* PRAB *a thumbs-up behind* DEVESH's *back*.

PRAB. Thank you...

KAJOL. Thank you for the opportunity, sir...

DEVESH *starts to usher them out*.

DEVESH (*to* CHELLAM). Happy now?

CHELLAM *gives him the finger*. PRAB *and* KAJOL *exit*.

CHELLAM. Do you enjoy being such an arsehole?

DEVESH. Day *and* night.

They start to passionately make out.

Scene Five

That night. KAJOL *gets ready for bed in their room while*
PRAB *works on the sewing machine, overlocking a pile of sari
blouses. The hubbub outside of neighbours chatting, street
sellers shouting and the hum and occasional blared horn of
traffic.*

PRAB. Come on, what's arse-licking if not lying?

KAJOL. It's not shooting your mouth off to your boss's son
about some fairytale. You bloody… *lunatic.*

PRAB. As long as I write something she likes, he'll go along
with it.

KAJOL. She wants something 'radical'. You can't do that.

PRAB. A story that will inspire ordinary people, light the spark
that lies dormant in every one of us.

KAJOL. That sounds like what *you* want.

PRAB. I could write something that wakes everyone up round
here.

KAJOL. Just write what *Devesh* wants and take the money.

PRAB. He says they want a new direction.

KAJOL. His dad's one of those saffron bebsayis. Visits temple
in a suit. Attends board meetings with a tilaka. What do you
think he'll do if he hears you've been fucking with the
Mahabharata?

PRAB. Chandi's not in the *Mahabharata* though.

KAJOL. Yes, I know. And if the Nags find out you'll be even
less employable than you are now.

PRAB. We could really shake up the jatra. Create a buzz.

KAJOL. Fine, do that. Chandi squabbling with her siblings,
defying her mother-in-law, running away to work in the big
city. Not Chandi inspiring a peasants' revolt, okay? You raise
their suspicions with this, they might *really* start digging.

PRAB. I'll be careful.

KAJOL. Careful? You've already lied to Devesh's face.

PRAB. If he asks about that I'll tell him Chandi was written out centuries ago. Erased from history.

KAJOL. So how come you know so much about her?

PRAB. ...I'll say my uncle was a porter at Hansraj College and overheard some of the lecturers talking about her.

KAJOL. Which uncle?

PRAB. Boloram.

KAJOL. Boloram's a deadbeat junkie.

PRAB. He was a good student when he was younger. Maybe if he'd had a break or two he could've made a decent life for himself.

KAJOL. I don't think so, Prab. I think he likes heroin too much. Also, I think your plan stinks.

PRAB. So what's your big idea?

KAJOL (*of their surroundings*). Keep our heads down and make enough to get out of this place. Like we agreed. And bonus, when the factory opens again, Mr Nag realises you're the best machinist in Kolkata and gives you a permanent contract.

PRAB. This jatra thing could be better.

KAJOL. Or it could be a lot worse. And definitely more risky.

PRAB. I can handle it.

KAJOL checks on Amba in her Moses basket, then goes to bed. PRAB *finishes the last of the blouses.*

And if Devesh likes what I come up with, he might ask me to write more.

He puts the final blouse on the pile. He gives Amba's Moses basket a rock.

KAJOL. Stop it, she's asleep.

Amba stirs and starts to cry.

Fuck's sake.

PRAB. Hey, hey there, it's okay, it's okay. Shhh. Shhh.

PRAB picks her up and starts to pace with her in his arms.
He hums to her – the song from Chellam and Devesh's jatra
about Draupadi. Amba starts to settle. KAJOL watches
them, drifting off to sleep. PRAB sits on the bed beside her,
Amba resting on his chest. He makes a few shadow puppets
on the wall.

So, Amba, storytime is a bit different today. We need to
imagine Chandi setting out in the world, meeting new people
– lots of new people. What kind of story do they want to see,
chotto? We know *some* of them want a tale that feels daring
and dangerous, but mainly makes them look good. We know
others want a story that says something people haven't heard
before. But then that really is dangerous. We like those
people more, don't we? But that could get us into a lot of
trouble... Okay. When Chandi calls, her friends answer.
Maybe *they're* calling her now? Why do they need her help?
What if there's this landowner, who starts pushing them
around...? What if he's called... Sengupta?

Scene Six

Two weeks later. CHELLAM sits reading in the back room at
Khub Bhalo factory. PRAB enters, carrying a plastic bag.

PRAB. Oh, sorry...

He goes to leave. CHELLAM puts down her book.

CHELLAM. You just got here.

PRAB. I'm early. I'll wait outside.

CHELLAM. You're not early, Devesh is late. He's always late.
If you stand around waiting for him we won't get anything
done.

PRAB....Oh. Okay. Yes.

Awkward beat.

CHELLAM (*of his bag*). Is it in there?

PRAB. Would you like to take a look?

CHELLAM. Tell me about it. Get me up to speed before his majesty arrives and starts picking holes in everything.

PRAB. Okay... Yes... Of course... Um... So, it's about this girl, Chandi...

CHELLAM. Yes, the mysterious daughter of Barbarik himself. Set the scene, for God's sake.

PRAB. It's set in the past – say, a few hundred years ago...

CHELLAM. That's so... *vague*.

PRAB. It's not really a historical piece. There's a blurring of real life and fantasy, so it doesn't need to be pinpointed in time.

CHELLAM. You're running with the fantasy elements, then?

PRAB. Yes. I mean. No...

CHELLAM. The whole point of this project was to get away from all this mystical bullshit and finally look at *real people's* lives.

PRAB. It is. In the ways that matter. As far as Chandi knows, she's just an ordinary girl, trying to make her way in the world. She's the role model *everyone* needs. She's... resourceful, loyal, intelligent, principled. And she knows there is no challenge she and her friends can't face, together.

CHELLAM. How old is she?

PRAB. Young.

CHELLAM. How young?

PRAB. Um...

CHELLAM. This is my part, yes?

PRAB. Late twenties?

CHELLAM. Great. And what does she want, what does she do?

PRAB. This is a story about Chandi and her friends witnessing the creation of a new, modern world.

CHELLAM. Okay...

PRAB. When we meet her, Chandi lives by her wits alone, in the forest, by the river with her animal friends.

CHELLAM. Sorry, what? Did you say 'animal friends'?

PRAB.... Yes.

CHELLAM. Don't tell me they can talk?

PRAB. They can talk.

CHELLAM. Oh fuck.

PRAB. Um... And... their land lies between the kingdoms of two brothers, Sengupta and Chandok Sri, as powerful and ambitious as each other. When Sengupta hears his little brother has a new venture, he's inspired by the friendly competition and vows to rise to the challenge.

CHELLAM. What new venture?

PRAB. They've always made their money allowing the animals to live on their lands while they collect taxes from them. They grow rice, maize, maybe keep some fruit trees. They're happy as long as the animals pay up in extra taxes whenever they fancy a new wing to one of their palaces, or the dowry for another wife. If not, they send their men to beat it out of them. But now suddenly Chandok Sri has cleared his fields, cut down all the forests. Cleared them of all animals except the biggest and strongest, and he's making them plant something new. A magical crop, whose fruit turns into money.

CHELLAM. Cotton?

PRAB. Could be.

CHELLAM. Tobacco?

PRAB. It can be harvested, stored, transported, and sold far across the sea, bringing Chandok Sri riches beyond his wildest dreams. Sengupta is apoplectic with rage that his baby brother is now richer than him. He orders his men to clear the animals from *his* fields. To clear the paddies, the maize and the forest. All the animals are driven out, except for the biggest and strongest who are hungry and desperate, and have no choice but to cultivate the stolen land.

CHELLAM. So where's Chandi in all this?

PRAB. She's forced into the mountains with the smaller animals, and at first they accept the new status quo. They find streams to fish in, and forage berries on the craggy surface of the mountains and try to build a new life for themselves.

CHELLAM. But all along they plot their revenge alongside Chandi?

PRAB. Er, well, no...

CHELLAM *thinks about this for a moment.*

CHELLAM. But it is a story about the Naxalites?

PRAB....No. No.

CHELLAM. The peasants fighting for land rights, a decent wage, dignity, all that?

PRAB. It's not political.

CHELLAM. The ravages of neoliberalism.

PRAB. It's actually, er, based on a long-lost story from the *Mahabharata*...

CHELLAM. Yeah, yeah, not – (*Bangs the table.*) 'political', but it's an allegory, right? The animals are poor little fuckers being pushed around by the big shits and Chandi embodies the spirit of social justice and change.

PRAB....That's a bit of a leap.

CHELLAM. Well, otherwise it's about some kid and a bunch of talking monkeys, so I think you should go with the allegory.

PRAB. You and… Mr Nag… mentioned you might be interested in exploring a… different direction?

CHELLAM. It's definitely that.

PRAB. But I think maybe you both have… a slightly… different idea of what… that… means.

CHELLAM. Let me put your mind at rest. He has no fucking idea what he means.

PRAB *laughs nervously.*

I was sick of Adhil and his sloppy bullshit, but you're the exact opposite. You're so buttoned up it's like you're wearing a straitjacket.

PRAB. I'm not sure I… [understand.]

CHELLAM. Devesh is sweet, underneath all that macho bullshit, okay? He has raw talent – you've seen him. He used to sneak off to watch the jatra when he was supposed to be studying. He could be a really great performer, one day. If only he wasn't up against his dad whispering in his ear about making the Forbes Indian Rich List.

PRAB. That's what I'm worried about.

CHELLAM. I get it. You don't want that voice whispering 'You're fired.'

PRAB. Yes.

CHELLAM. What you need to understand about Devesh is he wouldn't know an allegory if it fucked him in the ear.

PRAB. Ah.

CHELLAM. So if you want to make this about a greedy landowner whose ambitions lead to death and destruction, I think you should go for it.

PRAB. Okay.

CHELLAM. Just let me do the talking.

PRAB. O… kay.

DEVESH *enters*.

DEVESH. Shit, new boy's keen.

CHELLAM. You're late.

DEVESH (*checking his watch*). No I'm not. (*To* PRAB.) Look at you, big man. Other side of the gates for a change. Most of them look alike, you know? This sort of, terrible desperation in the eyes. Certain *needy* smell. But you're... different.

PRAB. Thank you...?

DEVESH. Are you out there in the morning with the others?

PRAB. ...Most days.

DEVESH (*to* CHELLAM). Crack of dawn. Seriously. Some of them must sleep out there. (*To* PRAB.) Have you ever done that?

PRAB. No.

DEVESH. I've had people try to bribe me, just for a shift. You wouldn't *believe* some of the freaky shit I've been offered. (*To* CHELLAM.) Mainly IOUs. Or My-Wife-Owes-You.

CHELLAM *is disgusted*.

(*To* PRAB.) How're you managing? Got a sideline or something?

PRAB. I do a bit of work at home. Tailoring, alterations.

DEVESH. That's some *entrepreneurial* spirit, right there.

PRAB. I've found it really helpful. Has made me much more efficient. I can complete thirty pieces an hour now, easy.

DEVESH. Your own machine?

PRAB. It's a rental.

DEVESH. Where did you get your start-up costs?

PRAB. A loan from the kabuliwala.

DEVESH. Shit, man. Bet those repayments are killing you.

PRAB.... We manage. My wife's excellent at budgeting.

CHELLAM. Shall we talk about consolidating his debts or shall we get on with the scenes?

DEVESH. Yes! The *play*. (*Of* PRAB*'s bag*.) Let's take a look.

PRAB *takes out the scripts and passes them around*.

CHELLAM (*to* DEVESH). We've finished casting. You're pond-dwelling toad number two.

DEVESH (*to* PRAB). Brave man, alone in a room with this firecracker. (*Weighing the script in his hands*.) So what's it about?

PRAB *looks anxiously at* CHELLAM.

CHELLAM. Lord Sengupta is a... visionary. A modern man in pursuit of progress.

DEVESH. Oh?

CHELLAM. Ambitious enough to reshape the world, wise enough to meet the toughest of decisions.

PRAB. Agonising decisions.

CHELLAM. We see the man behind the crown.

DEVESH. That's me. Sengupta? Handsome? Witty? Good fighter?

PRAB. All those things.

DEVESH (*to* PRAB). So who are you?

PRAB. I'll read Arun.

DEVESH (*flicks through*). Wait... He's a... monkey?

PRAB. Yeah.

DEVESH (*bursts out laughing*). If you're happy with that, my friend.

CHELLAM. There are a variety of animals in the play.

DEVESH. So we have a Disney Schmisney hit on our hands.

CHELLAM (*to* DEVESH). You've played Hanuman.

DEVESH. Yes, but he's a *god*. (*To* PRAB.) Is this guy a god?

PRAB. Just an ordinary monkey.

DEVESH. Wow. Dream role, my friend. Okay, let's go.

They begin to read.

CHELLAM (*as Chandi*). The forest is so beautiful, this time of year. The leaves so thick above my hut, the sun casts shadow puppets on my walls. Now is the time to swim, and play, and rest.

PRAB (*as Arun*). Hello, Chandi.

CHELLAM (*as Chandi*). Good morning, Arun.

PRAB (*reading the stage directions*). He grabs a banana from her bag.

CHELLAM (*as Chandi*). Hey, that's my lunch! (*Reading stage directions.*) He runs off, she chases after him. She manages to grab his tail and they fall to the floor, laughing. (*As Chandi.*) What's this stuff on your fur...?

PRAB (*as Arun*). I can't see anything. (*Reading stage directions.*) He turns around, trying to see his own back, and falls over again.

CHELLAM (*reading stage directions*). He winces as Chandi cleans his fur. (*As Chandi.*) Feels strange... Sticky... I know what this is. It's that special tree sap. (*Coming out of character, to* PRAB.) *Oh*, it's rubber!

PRAB (*as Arun*). There are barrels and barrels piled up at the edge of Chandok Sri's land.

CHELLAM (*as Chandi*). I've told you not to go there.

PRAB (*as Arun*). I was having a great time hopping from one to the other, but one of them tipped and splashed me. It was full / of this stuff.

DEVESH. Are these two fucking or something?

PRAB. No. God... *No*.

DEVESH. And where's Sengupta? Having a wank somewhere?

CHELLAM (*to* DEVESH). Your opening scene's coming up, baby. You have an *amazing* entrance. (*To* PRAB.) Right?

PRAB *nods*.

PRAB. Lord Sengupta makes his mark from the *off*.

CHELLAM. Let's go back... Okay?

DEVESH. Fine.

CHELLAM (*as Chandi*). The forest is so beautiful, this time of year.

Scene Seven

PRAB *rattles off a pile of sari blouses at the sewing machine in his and* KAJOL*'s room later that night.*

KAJOL. She's fucking Nag's son. You can't trust her.

PRAB. She says it's okay. I shouldn't hold back. She knows the best way to sell tickets is to connect with ordinary people.

KAJOL. But we are ordinary people. And she's not.

PRAB. She's really down-to-earth, you know? I think you'd like her.

KAJOL. Not as much as you do.

PRAB. Are you... jealous?

KAJOL. Fuck off.

PRAB. Because she's *way* out of my league.

KAJOL. Oh, is that right...?

PRAB. Joking, I'm joking.

Beat.

Come on... You're the one who wanted me to do this.

KAJOL. Do it, don't enjoy it.

PRAB. I'm lucky, really. Have the ideal test audience in Amba.

KAJOL. Ore baba, you're competing for her attention with a Mickey Mouse night light.

PRAB. Babies understand human emotion without any filter. Things are either good or really fucking terrible. There's no way you can bullshit her.

KAJOL. Don't rope Amba into this, alright?

PRAB takes out a carefully folded bill from his pocket and hands it to KAJOL. She unfolds it with amazement.

A thousand taka…?

PRAB. And they'll pay me more when I finish the draft. They liked what I came up with. Devesh thinks his dad will keep up the funding.

KAJOL carefully puts the money away.

KAJOL. We'll pay the kabuliwala, give some to Ma, and save the rest.

PRAB. Let's see if they have ilish at the market.

KAJOL (*of the money he just gave her*). That's for our deposit.

PRAB. That's a lot of ilish.

KAJOL. We'll get there. A friend of Archana says a flat's come up in her building.

PRAB. We can't afford a place in Dum Dum.

KAJOL. Rents are low right now. They'd rather someone move in quickly than lose it to squatters. We could at least see it.

PRAB. I don't want you to get your hopes up.

KAJOL. Oh God forbid we have any hope, any *dreams*.

PRAB. Your ma will miss Amba.

KAJOL. The air is cleaner over there. You can see the river. There are two good schools nearby.

PRAB. We don't have to think about that yet.

KAJOL. It will come around sooner than you think. Don't you want that for Amba?

PRAB. This is no different to what we grew up with.

KAJOL. And look at us.

PRAB. I thought you were happy?

KAJOL. I didn't say we were happy, I said we had *dreams*.

PRAB. Fuck. Okay.

KAJOL. You cavort around with your jatra buddies, I think of ways to make our lives better. Make a decent future for our daughter.

PRAB. That's not fair.

KAJOL. You know what I've been doing the three hours you've with been with your... *jatra* friends?

PRAB. It's been more like two / hours.

KAJOL. *Three* hours. I cleaned the Basus' place, the Guptas' place, the *Das*guptas'. I haggled over half a pound of rice, a bag of moong dal and four kohlrabis at Koley Market. And did an hour at the centre. All with Amba on my back.

PRAB. You went to the centre?

KAJOL. Ajanta asked me to help out.

PRAB. What if Nag hears?

KAJOL. Nag isn't bothered about a bunch of women doing social work.

PRAB. He would be if he knew you're all communists.

KAJOL. *Community Organisers*. Then I came home and finished the blouses left in your pile –

PRAB. You didn't have to do that.

KAJOL. I don't mind. As long as we agree we're working towards the same thing. As long as all of this is for a reason.

Space of our own. Space to *breathe*. Space for Amba to…
thrive.

Beat.

Nikhil was at the centre. Says he's looking for work.

PRAB. He's back?

KAJOL. There was a bust-up in his group about accepting NGO
funding and he was on the side of autonomy. He quit. Loads
of autonomy when you're unemployed. He was asking if
there's anything going at Khub Bhalo.

PRAB. If this works out maybe I'll be able to help.

KAJOL. You need to stay away from him.

PRAB. Oh come on.

KAJOL. That's our old life, Prab.

PRAB. I meant a coffee.

KAJOL. He's blacklisted in every factory in the city. You can't
be seen with him.

PRAB. You were with him at the centre?

KAJOL. He wasn't there to work. He was hungry. They've got
people queueing up in the morning before they even open.
They're doing five hundred food parcels a week, two
hundred meals every day.

PRAB. Was he okay?

KAJOL. Honestly, I don't know.

Beat.

PRAB. Okay… Let's see the place in Dum Dum.

   KAJOL *pats him affectionately on the chest. He holds her in*
   his arms. They start to kiss. Then Amba stirs in her Moses
   basket and starts crying.

KAJOL. It's like she has some sort of sixth sense.

PRAB. You mean like a... special power?

KAJOL. Oh shut up.

PRAB *picks up Amba and starts to hum and rock her.*

I'm going to wash up.

KAJOL *goes to leave.*

Just get her settled, okay? She needs sleep, not epic tales.

PRAB. Okay, okay...

KAJOL *exits.* PRAB *settles on the bed with Amba in his arms. He starts to make shadow puppets on the wall, conjuring up the world of Chandi for the two of them to enter.*

So, chotto. Where did we get to? Yes, that's right, it's called a 'cliffhanger'. And our characters are in the mountains so it's a really big one. They can see all the way down to the plantation where their friends now toil for Sengupta on the lands they used to call home. This new work for Sengupta looks back-breaking, in every weather, from blazing hot sunshine to freezing wind and hail. If the working animals slow down or try to rest, Sengupta's men beat them. They're paid for their time, not what they produce. The little animals can see everything from their vantage point in the mountains. The land is changing. Whatever Sengupta has planted has made the ground hard and dry. Chandi sends the falcons out to explore further. They return squawking and distressed. The top layer of earth has worn away, carried off by the wind and the monsoon rains, leaving dry, arid earth that cannot soak up the water. The falcons could see the river rising and rising. The forests that used to surround the land have been cleared so it lies unprotected. Chandi can see disaster looming, but what can she do? She's just a girl. Her friends are only small. But we both know when Chandi calls, her friends answer. And this is the biggest challenge they've ever faced. But should they overcome it? Or is it more powerful if they fail...?

Scene Eight

PRAB, CHELLAM *and* DEVESH *are lost in Chandi's magical and righteous world as they rehearse the new scenes.*

CHELLAM (*as Chandi*). You must believe us, Lord Sengupta. The banks of the river have burst and the flood is heading this way.

DEVESH (*as Sengupta*). Nice try, Chandi. You think I'd be so foolish as to abandon my own lands over the witterings of a hysterical woman?

PRAB (*as Arun*). The falcons have seen it with their own eyes. Why would we lie?

DEVESH (*as Sengupta*). Jealousy. Trickery. Maybe it's harder up in the mountains than you expected and you'd like to worm your way back into my kingdom?

CHELLAM (*as Chandi*). Then please, just let us tell our friends so they can escape.

DEVESH (*as Sengupta*). Oh-ho! So that is your devious plan. You want to lure your friends away?

PRAB (*as Arun*). They have a right to leave.

DEVESH (*as Sengupta*). If they choose to, of course. They are paid labourers, not slaves.

CHELLAM (*as Chandi*). Take us to them.

DEVESH (*as Sengupta*). Come down to the pens and tell them the news.

CHELLAM (*as Chandi*). They will want to *survive*.

PRAB (*as Arun*). Bapu! Gurvinder!

CHELLAM (*as Chandi*). Aziz! Priya! Time is short. Bring whatever you can carry. We must go.

PRAB (*as Arun*). She said we must go! Hurry.

DEVESH (*reading stage directions*). Sengupta starts to laugh.

CHELLAM (*as Chandi*). What have you done to them?

DEVESH (*as Sengupta*). I've given them somewhere safe to sleep at night.

CHELLAM. They sleep in filthy hovels.

DEVESH (*as Sengupta*). Provided three nutritious meals a day.

CHELLAM (*as Chandi*). Gruel and bugs…?

DEVESH (*as Sengupa*). *Guaranteed* gruel and bugs. Maybe they prefer that to the… lavish fish suppers that are only a promise from you.

CHELLAM (*as Chandi, to the animals*). I know you're scared, but you're strong, and… we're even stronger together. Don't listen to him.

DEVESH. This is really fucking depressing, my friend.

The spell is broken and PRAB *is back in the back room of Khub Bhalo with* DEVESH *and* CHELLAM.

PRAB. Oh…

CHELLAM. It's not depressing, it's tragic. It's a realistic reflection of what ordinary people are up against.

DEVESH. Baba just signed a contract with the biggest brand of sportswear in the world. Snatched it right from under PMC and Evergreen's noses, too. Those bastards can eat our shit. Khub Bhalo is back in business, baby. Ordinary people are about to get *paid*.

PRAB. That's excellent news.

DEVESH. Yes it is 'excellent news'. So read the room, my friend. Bin this tragic bullshit. No one wants to see this.

PRAB. What were you thinking?

DEVESH. We need something uplifting. Something full of fucking hope.

PRAB. Okay, I can work up something else.

CHELLAM (*to* PRAB). You're going to change it? Just like that?

DEVESH. He can be flexible. You should try it. And that's why... he has a... new *permanent* contract at Khub Bhalo.

PRAB. I... Do I...? Really...?

DEVESH. Yes. Fuck it. You can have a promotion. How'd you like to be a line manager?

PRAB. I... Thank you, thank you so much. You won't regret this.

DEVESH. And there's a job for your wife too.

PRAB. My wife?

DEVESH. If she wants it?

PRAB. Yes, yes, she would *delighted*.

DEVESH. We reopen Monday. Everyone will want to celebrate their first payday by heading to the jatra at the weekend. Win-win, my friend.

CHELLAM (*to* PRAB). Everyone has a price. Looks like you just found yours.

DEVESH. You're the one always going on about the jatra being a 'collaboration'.

CHELLAM. Yes, not *capitulation*.

DEVESH. Give him some credit. Prab's a clever guy. (*To* PRAB.) You'll come up with something great, I know you will.

CHELLAM (*to* PRAB). Here are my opinions. You don't like them? I've got others. You're like a poor-quality meme.

Scene Nine

A few days later. DEVESH *unlocks the door to the apartment in Dum Dum, and enters with* KAJOL *and* PRAB.

DEVESH. Bedroom one, through there, bedroom two, there. That one's smaller – space for a single bed and a cot for little Amba if you like. Bathroom. Power shower.

PRAB. 'Power shower'…?

DEVESH. You will love it, my friend. It's like having a wash and a massage at the same time. (*To* KAJOL.) Even more fun with two.

Awkward laughter.

PRAB. Is it an immersion heater?

DEVESH. How the fuck should I know?

PRAB. Just wondering what the bills will be like.

DEVESH. Hot water's included. I've paid the deposit and first three months up front.

KAJOL. Really?

DEVESH. You can move in today. I wouldn't be wasting my time showing you around otherwise. What am I – an estate agent?

More laughter.

KAJOL. This is very generous of you.

DEVESH. I like to help out where I can. And I usually can.

KAJOL. It's bigger than I expected.

DEVESH. But a public urinal is bigger than your place.

KAJOL*'s offended, but* PRAB *gives her a warning look. She forces a smile.*

KAJOL.…Least it doesn't smell like one.

DEVESH (*to* KAJOL). What I want to know is, is he always so serious? (*Impression of Prab.*) How can you stand it?

KAJOL. Ohhh… He has his moments.

DEVESH (*to* PRAB). I'd like to see you let your hair down one of these days. Unclench those buttcheeks.

He slaps PRAB *on the back.*

PRAB. Maybe after a power shower?

DEVESH. Oh-ho, was that a joke…? That *was* a joke – yes! (*To* KAJOL*; Prab impression.*) He's very serious about his writing too.

KAJOL. He isn't serious when he's at home.

DEVESH. Oh no?

KAJOL. He's a complete joker with us, aren't you?

PRAB. Um…

DEVESH (*to* KAJOL). Take a look around.

KAJOL. Thank you.

KAJOL *exits.*

PRAB. We'll pay you back. Every paisa.

DEVESH. I'll take it straight out of your wages. Keep it nice and simple.

PRAB…. You've thought of everything.

DEVESH. All set for Monday? Back on the shop floor after all this time.

PRAB. Can't wait.

DEVESH. Your own team.

PRAB. Big responsibility.

DEVESH. Be able to stretch your legs, go for a piss whenever you want. Play favourites with your wife now she's on the team.

DEVESH *winks at* PRAB*, who manages a laugh.* DEVESH *jangles the keys to the flat.*

Enjoy, my friend.

PRAB. It will be so good to have our own space. Thank you.

DEVESH. And one night a week you all get to go back to
Didima's.

PRAB.... Sorry...?

DEVESH. My cousin's moved to a new place across the road
from Chellam, so her apartment isn't so... *discreet* any more.

PRAB. Oh...

DEVESH. He's an ambitious little shit. He'll have word all
around town before I have time to pull my trousers up.

Awkward beat which PRAB fills with awkward laughter.

Oh yeah, it's funny, is it? Is your family like that?

PRAB. Um...

DEVESH. Everyone thinks Baba's a class-A bastard, but seem
to think me and Ma are spared his bastarding.

PRAB.... It must be really... tough for you.

DEVESH. I'm not like him. He's a street hustler made good.
He's never had the chance to cultivate an appreciation of the
arts like me. I'm grateful he's given me that, but there's a
price. I have to play the 'shrewd businessman' to the letter.
There are backstabbers everywhere.

PRAB. In a way, it shows what a... confident performer you
are.

DEVESH. Don't bullshit me.

PRAB. No, no, I wouldn't.

DEVESH. I'm no Chellam Dey, but I am a grafter.

PRAB. Totally.

DEVESH. She only has to think about her lines, I have to do
that *and* think about funding the whole thing.

PRAB. It's a... huge responsibility.

DEVESH. It is. So. Keys.

DEVESH *dangles them out to* PRAB, *who hesitates, then takes them.* DEVESH *leaves.* KAJOL *re-enters.*

KAJOL. Has he gone? I didn't even say goodbye.

Amba starts to cry from the next room. PRAB *goes to check on her.*

Scene Ten

PRAB *lifts the crying Amba from the Moses basket in the bedroom and starts to rock her. He puts on the familiar night light.*

PRAB. Look, who's this, chotto? See? Mickey's here. Just like always. See? See?

He sits on the bed, propping her up in one arm, and starts to make shadow puppets on the walls. Amba cries harder.

Oh no. Poor Amba. Poor little one. What's wrong? What is it? Are you too hot? Is it hot in here?

He loosens her clothing.

Is that better?

She continues to cry.

Hey, hey, hey…

He sniffs her bottom. Nothing.

What is it? Is it too dark?

He cracks open the door and lets in some light from the living room. Amba cries harder.

Too light?

He closes the door again. Covers the night light with the edge of the sheet. An eerie glow is cast across the room.

Too much… space…?

He tightens the swaddling cloth around her.

Let's tuck you in, shall we? Just like when you first arrived in the world. Is that better? Hey, chotto? How does that feel? Cosy, warm?… Safe…?

Amba's cries quieten. PRAB *stands, listening for a moment.*

It's so quiet. So… Where were we? Where did we leave brave young Chandi and her friends? Arun and Aziz and all the little animals? They were arguing with Sengupta about the flood, to no avail. They're all about to be overrun by the watery depths. Chellam likes that ending. Says I'm a sell-out if I change it.

Amba stirs and starts to cry again.

Oh, you think so too, chotto? So what *should* they do? Run? Swim? Leave for the mountains? But Sengupta can't have Chandi and her friends trying to build something new for themselves, because what if it works? What if they render him… obsolete…? Devesh doesn't want to hear that. That's a story he can't afford for *anyone* to tell.

Amba cries louder.

I'm sorry, chotto. Maybe your baba isn't as brave as he thought…

Continued crying.

…But maybe I need to think like Chandi. Who is more clever, or brave, or cunning than her?

Thoughtful gurgle from Amba. He holds her closer, pats her back gently. Amba starts to drop off to sleep.

And she *always* has a plan.

Scene Eleven

Two days later. PRAB *walks out of the factory in his overalls in place of Devesh, clipboard in hand, mobile phone between his shoulder and ear. The machines in the factory have whirred into life and can be heard from inside.*

PRAB. Work today, work today. Big new order. (*Pointing at some of the expectant workers.*) You, you, Budhedev. Yes, you. We need three more machinists. Yes, yes, come on, come on.

Beat.

No – sorry. No work for you. You have to be fourteen or older – you know the law. How old is he? What?

Some of the new workers are children. The sound of the machines becomes deafening.

PRAB *meets with* DEVESH *in the back room after his shift, that evening.*

DEVESH. His ma came to us on her knees, begging Baba to take him on. 'Please bhai, he's a good worker, give him a chance, he'll prove it.' They moved here from their tiny latrine of a village to find work but ended up all the way out in Hatgachha. Her husband died last year. Left her with two lakhs of debt. He was a drinker and a gambler. Owed money to every goondah in town. What do you think she had to do to keep up those payments, my friend? How do you think she managed to stop them breaking her children's legs and taking what's left of her honour?

PRAB. ...It must have been very hard for her.

DEVESH. It's still *hard*, we've just made it less impossible. What sort of man would he be to say no to her? What would she have done if he had? Hobbled her kids' feet herself? Sent them to Howrah to beg for a few paisa every day? Now she has a little room to breathe. A tiny bit of dignity. But you'd have us take it away again.

PRAB. ...No.

DEVESH. You tell her there's no place for her son at the factory.

PRAB. I… That's not what / I meant…

DEVESH. I'll explain to Baba. Allocate the boy's work to someone else in finishing. Who deserves it?

PRAB.… Your father is a… kind man.

DEVESH. Tough decisions have to be made. And all the time the unionists and the reds sit on their backsides and try to undermine him, judging his every move.

Long beat.

PRAB. I've noticed the boy doesn't have… gloves.

DEVESH. So we should provide him with some?

PRAB.… Yes.

DEVESH. And the other children?

PRAB.… Yes.

DEVESH. Health and safety.

PRAB. And… I would like to line-manage them.

DEVESH. Oh…? You see yourself as some sort of Pied Piper? Only just started and you're already looking to take on more responsibilities?

PRAB. They're finishing the clothes my team are working on so it streamlines things if I take them on too.

DEVESH.… Got you. Like it, my friend. Showing some *initiative*.

PRAB. Just makes more sense.

DEVESH. I'm glad you're taking this attitude, my friend. We're connected, aren't we? My first post managing my own factory. Your first post managing the fuckers on the shop floor. Your star rises with mine.

PRAB.…I'm very grateful for all the opportunities you've given me.

DEVESH. I have another job for you. Some fucker's tipped off the unions and they've got some firingi journalist sniffing around. Sort it.

DEVESH *slaps him on the back.*

Scene Twelve

PRAB *and* KAJOL *are in the living room of the duplex.* PRAB *has just returned home from work – he's maybe changing out of his work clothes into kurta pyjama or doing some prep for dinner.* KAJOL *holds a sleeping Amba, resting on her shoulder, as she folds laundry with one hand.*

PRAB. I used to think we were on an… upward trajectory. (*Motions.*) We were here, with the worst of the shit behind us. Progress was inevitable, was already happening. People were waking up and realising they had a right to demand more. Just a… fair wage, a roof over their heads…

KAJOL. Not just you.

PRAB. Is that too much? Were we asking for too much?

KAJOL.…It's different now.

PRAB. I had coffee with Nik.

KAJOL.…Why…?

PRAB. He told me all about Maharashtra. Beed. The cane-cutters he was working with. Every other woman he met – every other woman in those fields, had had a hysterectomy.

KAJOL.…There were… older woman working the fields?

PRAB. No, no no, women in their thirties, in their *twenties*. No toilets, you see? Nowhere to change your underwear… No rest for anyone suffering from period pain… So – simple solution. Remove their wombs. And you have a reliable one hundred per cent model worker. One who can put in longer hours, take less breaks.

KAJOL.... But... no one... made them...? I mean... They weren't forced?

PRAB. It was their rational choice. How to provide best for the children they'd managed to have. How to keep a roof over their heads. That's just common sense, right?

Beat.

Nik tried to sign them up for a class action but no one wanted to be blacklisted. And he was telling me, and I was thinking 'Fuck me, this is as bad as it gets.' But then I remembered, I'm the one trying to work out how to make the shop floor more comfortable for children. For *children*. And I guess, thank God they're not *our* children...?

KAJOL. Which kids are working at Khub Bhalo?

PRAB. Protham. Jyoti. Sumit...

KAJOL. Sumit Dutta? Indranil and Deepa's son?

PRAB. Yes, him.

KAJOL. Deepa works at the factory too.

PRAB. So that's okay then?

KAJOL. They took out that loan for the auto. This is probably a short-term thing until it's paid off. And now they've got you looking out for him.

PRAB. Great. So I'm a sticking plaster on an open wound?

KAJOL. What else are they supposed to do? What else are *you* supposed to do?

PRAB.... Something... *Anything...*

KAJOL. Stage a demonstration? Occupy the shop floor?

PRAB. I'm going to speak to everyone they've laid off. Tell them they've got no prospect of work as !ong as kids are doing their jobs.

KAJOL. So turn the workers against each other?

PRAB. Make them see they can only get their jobs back and keep their kids safe if we work together.

KAJOL. Khub Bhalo have their biggest order for years. Nag's worked out how to undercut his rivals, people who've been swiping contracts from them this whole time. Making sure *we've* been out of work, *we've* been hungry, *we've* been desperate. Now the factory's open and running, the factory's full. And you think some ex-staff sulking outside will make Nag give it all up? You think the families who are finally making some money, some reliable money, are going to thank you for that?

PRAB (*of the duplex*). Has this place gone to your head? Sounds like you've switched sides.

KAJOL. There's only one shitty side, Prab.

PRAB. The union are going to picket. They think they have fifty per cent.

KAJOL. You can't get involved.

PRAB. Devesh has told me to speak to them. He's given me a budget. See if they'll take a bribe to call it off. He says it's bad for PR.

KAJOL.…So that's what you have to do.

PRAB. He said my 'old friends' will find it easier to swallow coming from me.

KAJOL.…So he has done some digging.

PRAB. I'm extra added value. Fastest overlocker *and* biggest backstabber in Kolkata.

KAJOL. He's testing your loyalty.

PRAB. I know that.

KAJOL. So make sure you pass.

PRAB. The staff who've been replaced by kids are like a coiled spring. They have to jump some time. What do they have to lose?

KAJOL. If they had any sense they'd move on, see if they have work at Evergreen or PMC. Or over the border.

PRAB. The never-ending search for a factory owner who won't screw them over.

KAJOL. It's not that simple.

PRAB. All they care about is profit. Just... zeros piling up on a screen.

KAJOL. But they need us to do the work.

PRAB. Until we're replaced with children. They'll always be cheaper.

KAJOL. A child cannot be a manager – exactly why you have to make sure you keep this job.

PRAB. Save myself?

KAJOL. ...I never demanded anything of you. This was your choice. Ma would have taken us in. It wouldn't have been easy but me and Amba would have managed. You could have joined Nikhil in Beed, done whatever you wanted.

PRAB. Don't say that.

KAJOL. We would have been okay.

PRAB. You and Amba are everything to me.

KAJOL. So act like it. If you walk away now, they'll never let you return to Khub Bhalo. The Nags will make sure every factory in the state knows you're a troublemaker. And how long has it taken for you to shrug off that reputation? What would happen if you had to wear it again? Not just us, hungry, on the street, or in Hatgachha. Amba too. There's no point in making some big statement unless you've got a chance of winning. And you don't.

PRAB. So many of our neighbours out of a job but you're at the centre, making sure their bellies are full. Doing Nag's work for him.

KAJOL. How is it Nag's work?

PRAB. Keeping everyone this side of outrage.

KAJOL. No, keeping them this side of *despair*.

PRAB. Least your conscience is clear.

KAJOL. I don't have time to pay attention to my conscience, Prab. I look after Amba, I do my ten hours at Khub Bhalo, I cover my share of the rent, and if I'm able to, I make sure our neigbours aren't going hungry. I put my efforts where I know I can make a difference.

Amba wakes up and starts to fuss. KAJOL *coos and rocks her.*

PRAB. You used to think we could do more.

KAJOL. I'm sorry we've turned out to be such a disappointment.

PRAB. Don't say that... I... *I* didn't mean that.

KAJOL. If you're floundering... *when* you are floundering. Think of Amba.

PRAB. ...Devesh wants me to lie to some journalist for him...

KAJOL. What will you say?

PRAB. I don't know.

KAJOL *hands Amba to him.*

KAJOL. Try and get her back to sleep? I need to check on the rice.

PRAB *rocks and fusses over Amba, pacing the floor to settle her. In the blink of an eye they're transported to Chandi's world, the shadow characters of* PRAB's *imagination surrounding them. They look up together, as a flock of a million falcons flies over them.*

Scene Thirteen

Next morning. PRAB is on the shop floor of Khub Bhalo, clipboard in hand. The clatter of the sewing machines is deafening. One of the falcons is still circling.

PRAB (*to one group of machinists, including* KAJOL). Eleven o'clock – Block A, take a break. Fifteen minutes, okay, make the most of it, people. Block B, get ready for an in-line inspection – Mr Nag will be here any minute.

The phone on the wall rings. PRAB answers while looking at paperwork, multitasking.

Khub Bhalo. Prab speaking.

More falcons circling. PRAB speaks to a JOURNALIST in New Delhi.

JOURNALIST. Hi, I'm Rita Solanki, I'm calling from Reuters.

PRAB. Oh.

JOURNALIST. Devesh Nag gave me this number?

PRAB. I'm sorry, I didn't realise the time. We're in the middle of a huge order here.

JOURNALIST. I've heard. Is this Prab Mitra, manager at Khub Bhalo?

PRAB. *Floor* manager. Sorry, which paper did you say you work for?

JOURNALIST. I'm not with a paper, I'm with an agency. Bigger reach. Mr Nag said you'd be happy to discuss these allegations about the use of child labour at your factory?

PRAB *glances at* KAJOL, *taking out her packed lunch from her handbag.*

PRAB. I can confirm they're completely untrue.

JOURNALIST. This must put you in such a difficult position. I know you were involved in so many campaigns with the Student Federation – tenants' rights, access to education for kids from scheduled castes. Really inspiring stuff. Now you're having to defend this?

PRAB. All the young people working here are fourteen years or older, fully permitted within the law.

DEVESH *enters. He smiles and waves at* PRAB, *pacing up and down past the machinists as if he owns the place, which he does.*

JOURNALIST. And of course the trade union members must be your friends and comrades – what do they think about the role you're playing in all of this?

PRAB. We have an open and transparent relationship with the staff union, of course.

JOURNALIST. We have eyewitnesses who claim they've seen children as young as eight going into the factory.

PRAB. Khub Bhalo is one of the few companies resilient enough to reopen, despite the recession. We have a lot of rivals who want to undermine us. They'd say anything.

JOURNALIST. You must be desperate to do absolutely *anything* in your power to help these poor kids?

PRAB. The auditors have a monthly visit from the factory, I mean, the factory has a monthly visit from auditors – they've already been since we reopened.

JOURNALIST. It must be hard to even identify what the right thing to do is. The pressure from the Nags must be unbelievable.

PRAB. The Nags are decent and fair bosses. They're quite generous.

JOURNALIST. They are to you. I doubt any of the machinists are living in duplexes in Dum Dum?

PRAB. Okay, thank you. I have to get back to work now.

JOURNALIST. There *is* something you can do for these kids.

The falcons are now a dark flock, swooping above him.

I've sent you a camera, a disposable one – in a yellow Jiffy bag.

PRAB *glances at* DEVESH *and tries to take the phone as far away from the shop floor as possible*.

Unmarked. Things like this turn up on my desk all the time. If I find myself with pictures from the shop floor, I'll have no way of knowing who took them.

Beat.

All we need is a photo or two and we could bury the Nags. Those kids are counting on you.

PRAB *hangs up, shaken*.

DEVESH. Sorted?

PRAB. Yes.

He quickly grabs his clipboard again and composes himself.

Block B, get ready for in-line inspection. Mr Nag wants to see your work.

DEVESH. No, no, it's fine. You've got everything in hand, here.

DEVESH *places a heavy hand on* PRAB*'s shoulder before exiting*.

Scene Fourteen

CHELLAM, PRAB *and* DEVESH *run through the reworked
ending of the jatra in the back room of the factory.*

DEVESH (*as Sengupta*). Chandi, Lord Krishna himself has
made me see you are every bit my equal. Long-lost sister, it
is my honour to welcome you into the fold. Today sees the
dawn of a new alliance.

CHELLAM (*as Chandi*). No, Lord Sengupta, whatever Krishna
pronounces, I profess my humble and ongoing servitude to
you. You remain closer to God than I will ever be.

PRAB (*as Arun*). Chandi, don't you understand, this means you
are a descendant of Krishna himself! You must take your
rightful place alongside Sengupta and Chandok Sri. This is
cause for unprecedented celebration. Lift me and all of your
friends up with you. This is a miracle.

CHELLAM (*as Chandi*). No, Arun. That would be a slur
against the gods themselves. All of you who aren't anointed
must drown in the watery depths. Go, feed the fishes, and
remember this is the way the world is and must always be.

DEVESH (*as Sengupta*). That's a bit much, Chandi.

CHELLAM (*as Chandi*). *Lord* Sengupta, I have learned all
I know about the heavy burden of power and responsibility
from you. I will take my new duties very seriously. Come,
hand me a sack and I will drown the baby animals myself.

PRAB. Those aren't the lines.

CHELLAM. You said this was an inspiring story. You said
Chandi was a bold and intelligent leader.

DEVESH. Lord Krishna himself says she is.

CHELLAM. And what if he hadn't? She and her weak little
friends all die? Adhil could have written this. Feudal bullshit.

PRAB. That's unfair.

CHELLAM. Unfair? You're talking to me about unfair? When
you want to tell the whole town that the only way this young

woman can achieve freedom and anything close to justice, is
by finding out she's related to the big-shit landowner? And
they both turn out to be descendants of God?

PRAB. I told you she was Barbarik's daughter from the start.

CHELLAM. I thought we were moving away from that?

DEVESH. Just try, for once in your life, not to overthink
everything?

CHELLAM. That's never been a problem for you.

PRAB. It's supposed to be aspirational. *Uplifting*.

DEVESH. Everyone coming to see this will have some money
in their pockets for the first time in months. Half of them will
be pissed.

CHELLAM. And you'll be playing Sengupta, on the big golden
throne.

DEVESH. Yeah.

CHELLAM. All this time I thought you were interested in
honing your craft. Turns out you've just been typecast all
along – the stupid rich bastard.

   DEVESH *slaps her.* PRAB *instinctively grabs* DEVESH *and
   pulls him away.*

PRAB. Don't.

CHELLAM (*to* DEVESH). See?

   DEVESH *slowly prises* PRAB*'s fingers off his shirt.*

DEVESH (*to* PRAB). I think you should let go, my friend. (*To*
CHELLAM.) There's an elephant in the room, here. You're
too old to play the main part. Everyone's too polite to say it.

   CHELLAM *looks to* PRAB*, but he's too scared to say
   anything.*

   I was at that new place behind Park Street last night. I saw
   a very talented young performer who really impressed me.

CHELLAM.... What new place...?

DEVESH. Starlight.

CHELLAM. That's a strip joint.

DEVESH. She would be a fantastic Chandi.

CHELLAM. You're disgusting.

DEVESH. She wouldn't make all this fuss. But then, she's not as... experienced as you.

CHELLAM *swallows her anger.*

CHELLAM (*to* PRAB). This is what you get for fucking monkeys.

DEVESH. Oh, what happened to your artistic alliance?

CHELLAM. He's an arsehole, same as the rest of you.

CHELLAM *grabs her cigarettes and goes outside to smoke.*

DEVESH (*to* PRAB). You need to stop by that kid Protham's place on the way home.

PRAB. Now? It's late.

DEVESH. It was close to midnight when that bitch was begging me to take him on. He hasn't been in work for over a week. She can explain herself.

PRAB.... He must be ill.

DEVESH. A few of them have been off. It's your job to know these things.

PRAB. Kids are bags of germs. One of them comes down with something, the rest fall like dominoes.

DEVESH. So give him a hankie and tell him to get back to work.

PRAB *exits. He stops to talk to* CHELLAM, *briefly and quietly, outside.*

CHELLAM. Sell-out.

PRAB. You don't think there's a way this ending could be seen as a... call-to-arms...?

CHELLAM. Exactly what a sell-out would say.

CHELLAM *lights a new cigarette with her spent one and glowers at him.* PRAB *exits.*

Scene Fifteen

PRAB *returns home to the duplex later that night.* KAJOL *is working on some blouses on the sewing machine.*

PRAB. What are you doing?

KAJOL. Archana had too much to get through so I said I'd take a few pieces.

PRAB. You've been at work all day. Get some rest.

KAJOL *laughs derisively.*

KAJOL. Don't want to risk it.

PRAB. What're you talking about?

KAJOL. I saw Protham's ma on the way to work this morning. Said I'd stop by with some moong dal later. Only thing I can stomach when I'm sick. But he's not sick. He's been at *school.*

PRAB. Good for him.

KAJOL. You're not surprised? How can they afford that? They live in Hatgachha.

PRAB. I gave them the money, okay?

KAJOL. I know you did, Prab. She told me everything. You think I'm such an idiot I wouldn't find out?

PRAB. It's not a secret. You could have asked.

KAJOL. I think it had better be a bloody secret, don't you? You want Devesh to find out you're stealing his staff away? With *his* money?

PRAB. He told me to use it on the strikers. He didn't say *how*. I cut a deal with them. It was enough for a full term for each of the kids at school. So now there are shifts free at the factory again.

KAJOL. And next term? You really think you can be their lifelong benefactor?

PRAB. I'll work that out when I come to it.

KAJOL. It's a hell of a lot less security than Devesh was offering. You don't think they'd rather be working than given handouts?

PRAB. It's an... investment.

KAJOL. One little act of charity and you think you're Bill Gates.

PRAB. Sorry I'm not a big-shot bebsayi like Devesh.

KAJOL. He's given us both work. You've got a promotion. We've got somewhere decent to live, for the first time in our lives. What sort of *idiot* jeopardises that? You think you're so fucking clever. Swanning around with all these romantic ideas in your head. Like you're... above everyone else.

PRAB. I never said that. I would never say that to you.

KAJOL. Do you want to end up in the slum with Protham and his family?

PRAB. You don't think we can do better than this? Some... shiny duplex we get to live in *part time*? When my boss isn't using it for his love nest.

KAJOL. It's only one evening a week.

PRAB. At least at your ma's place we didn't panic every time we spilled something.

KAJOL. I just want to keep the place tidy.

PRAB. He's put us in a cage – fuck, I'm a performing monkey in his show.

KAJOL. Amba's grown out of all her clothes. I went to the mall today and I bought everything she needed. I chose things that were practical but I also chose things that I liked. Nice things. *New* things. And I didn't have to put anything back after the woman rang them up at the till. Do you know how that felt?

PRAB. Like a caged bird being fed?

KAJOL. Fuck you. You stupid, fucking bastard. We work our arses off making these clothes, don't we deserve them for Amba?

PRAB. What happens when Devesh ends things with his girlfriend? Minute he gets married we'll be out on the street.

KAJOL. He'll always have a mistress. He's that sort of guy.

PRAB. Sounds like he's your new hero.

KAJOL. I just need someone who can keep his word.

KAJOL *finishes the piece she's working on. She hands him a rucksack.*

PRAB. What's this?

KAJOL. If we're lucky you'll just be blacklisted like Nikhil. If not, you'll go missing one day and we'll never find the body. I don't want to take any chances.

PRAB.... You're throwing me out...?

KAJOL. We both need some space to think.

PRAB. Where am I supposed to go?

KAJOL. I don't know. You're the genius, aren't you?

PRAB *exits.* KAJOL *starts to cry.*

Scene Sixteen

PRAB *enters the back room of the factory. The hum and clatter of machines of staff on the night shift rattle through the walls from the shop floor next door.* PRAB *takes a blanket from his bag and rolls it out on the floor to create a makeshift bed. He lies down and lets go, starting to cry.* DEVESH *enters, agitated, and grabs a first-aid box from the shelves.*

DEVESH. What are you doing here? Bhavan's on shift tonight.

PRAB. I'm sorry, I needed somewhere to stay / tonight.

DEVESH. Can you drive?

PRAB. Er…

DEVESH. *Can you drive?*

PRAB. Yes, yes, I can.

DEVESH. You need to go to Medical College and drop him off at the entrance to emergency admissions.

PRAB. Who…?

DEVESH *(handing him the first-aid box)*. Find the morphine.

DEVESH *exits.* PRAB *does as he's told.* DEVESH *returns, holding a body wrapped in a blanket.*

There's a car parked on Eden Gardens.

DEVESH *hands the body to* PRAB.

PRAB. Did you hit a dog or something…?

DEVESH. We don't have time for this.

PRAB. Who is it?

PRAB *uncovers the figure. He's shocked to find one of the child workers – Protham, injured and unconscious.*

DEVESH. You don't take a dog to A and E. Shape up. I can't go – they might recognise me.

PRAB. What… what happened to him…?

DEVESH. It's his own fault. Told them not to touch the zigzag machines.

PRAB. But I thought he... [didn't work here any more]?

DEVESH. What?

PRAB. He hasn't been in for over a week.

DEVESH. He's been sneaking off to school, then crawling back here for the night shift. Stupid little shit must be delirious. I'll bring the car round, you carry him out. (*Of the first-aid box.*) If he wakes up, give him another shot. Otherwise he'll start screaming the place down again.

DEVESH *exits.*

PRAB. It's alright, it's alright. It's going to be alright.

PRAB *puts the boy on his makeshift bed, takes out the camera given to him by the journalist and quickly takes some photos of the boy and his injuries.*

You're going to be alright.

He takes the boy in his arms again and holds him tight, rocking him as if he were his own.

It's going to be alright. It's going to be alright. It's going to be...

Lights down.

End of Part One.

PART TWO

Scene Seventeen

Later that week, evening. A pop-up jatra stage outdoors at a big expo in Kolkata. The opening performance of the jatra.
DEVESH, CHELLAM *and* PRAB *have reached the final scene. It's been a rough show and the audience are noisy and restless, regularly interrupting with heckles and abuse.*

DEVESH (*as Sengupta*). Chandi, Lord Krishna himself has made me see you are every bit my equal. Long lost sister, it is my honour to welcome you into the fold. Today sees the dawn of a new alliance.

AUDIENCE MEMBER 1. Don't trust him, he's a fucking vampire!

DEVESH *glowers at the audience.*

CHELLAM (*as Chandi*). Lord Sengupta, I humbly accept your generosity, and pledge to use my position to uplift the weak and vulnerable everywhere.

AUDIENCE MEMBER 1. You taking the piss? A kid just lost his arm!

AUDIENCE MEMBER 2. Let them have it, sister.

DEVESH *glowers at the audience.*

DEVESH (*as Sengupta*). Together we will be the benevolent leaders our people need. Sister, we will ensure equality and justice spread throughout our lands as surely as the sun's rays warm the soil.

CHELLAM *manages to remain poised and focused despite the growing rage in the audience.*

CHELLAM (*as Chandi*). Arun, come, you have a new home in my court.

AUDIENCE MEMBER 1. While the rest of us starve. Lazy, greedy fuckers!

AUDIENCE MEMBER 2. Yeah, you bastards.

DEVESH (*as Sengupta*). Come, sister, you will be an inspiration to the women of this land.

AUDIENCE MEMBERS. Shut up, you cunt. Arsehole. Sister-fucker.

CHELLAM (*as Chandi*). Arun, let us take our rightful place alongside Lord Sengupta himself. We will never be hungry or scared again. Together with Sengupta we will protect everything we hold dear.

AUDIENCE MEMBER. What *he* holds dear!

AUDIENCE MEMBER 2. Whores, whiskey and cocaine!

CHELLAM (*as Chandi*). Here I am: Chandi. A free spirit with a new purpose. See how the gold of my throne reflects the sunlight shining on the faces of my people. My friends here to guide me. The song of hope and freedom rings true across our kingdom.

PRAB *turns up the amp for* CHELLAM*'s microphone as takes her seat beside* DEVESH.

(*Singing.*) Come sing! Of love and freedom,
Oh, a new dawn across our land
Lifted from the lowly gutter
A beacon of hope, we walk hand in hand.

AUDIENCE MEMBER 1. Lies! What freedom?

AUDIENCE MEMBER 2. We're still living in the fucking gutter.

PRAB *ducks just in time as an empty Coke bottle is hurled onto stage.*

The shouting and jeering gets louder. Cans and bottles are thrown onto the stage. PRAB *shields* CHELLAM *from another bottle, filled with urine.*

PRAB (*to jatra audience*). Stop it.

DEVESH (*to jatra audience*). Who threw that? Stand up, you coward. Fuck you all. You think I won't find out?

AUDIENCE MEMBER 1 (*shouting*). Fuck you! Arsehole!

DEVESH (*to jatra audience*). You think you'll be safe going home tonight? Going to *sleep*? My people will find you and you'll regret this.

AUDIENCE MEMBER 2. Fuck your mother.

CHELLAM (*singing*). Come sing! Of love and freedom,
Oh, a new dawn across our land!
Lifted from the lowly gutter,
A beacon of hope, we walk hand in hand.
Come sing!

A can is thrown and glances off CHELLAM. PRAB *quickly shields her. Another hits* DEVESH *in the head – he realises he's bleeding.*

AUDIENCE MEMBER 1 *clambers onto the stage, cheered on by the rest of the crowd.*

AUDIENCE MEMBER 1 (*to jatra audience*). Hello, Kolkata, how are you doing tonight? Hello to all the belt-tighteners, the eat-or-heaters, the out-of-workers, the down-on-your-luckers. Hello to the fucked over, hello to the cold, the desperate, the fucking hungry, put-up-and-shut-uppers. Welcome to the afflicted, welcome to the flat broke, welcome to the broken and the wretched and the needy. You're only welcome here if you're on your *knees*, brothers and sisters.

The crowd whoops, spurring her on. CHELLAM *and* PRAB *look on in astonishment.*

But that's not us, is it? *We're* not boot-lickers. We're not arse-kissers. Are we? Louder! At the back – let me hear you. Up there – let me hear you. Come on. We're not, are we? And *we* aren't the ones getting fucked up tonight? Right? Yeah! You, over there, yes, you. You can do better than that. Louder! Let me hear you. Give it to me. This is for Protham! Inquilab Zindabad! Inquilab Zindabad! Inquilab…

DEVESH *manages to compose himself and grabs* AUDIENCE MEMBER 1 *under the arms, manhandling her off the stage.*

...Zindabad!

The fury and resentment of the audience explodes into a riot. Smoke, noise and chaos.

CHELLAM. Come on, let's *go*.

More bottles, cans and jeers. PRAB *shields* CHELLAM *and they exit quickly.*

Scene Eighteen

PRAB *and* CHELLAM *enter the back room of Khub Bhalo, escaping the riot outside.* PRAB *quickly locks the door behind them and they both pull down the blinds before turning on the lights.*

PRAB. Did you see what happened to Devesh?

CHELLAM. Don't worry about him. Nag has people in every corner of the city. If anyone so much as messes up his baby's hair they'll wish they were never born.

PRAB. ...Every corner?

CHELLAM. Yes.

PRAB. Including Dum Dum?

CHELLAM. Are you kidding? It's the seat of his property empire.

PRAB. ...Right. Of course it is. Soon as it quietens down I'll get you home. And, I mean... I'll go home too.

CHELLAM. We just dodged bottles of piss together. You can loosen up a bit. Looks like you're stuck with me for now, so you can tell me all about plotting that call-to-arms. You devious bastard.

PRAB. I thought it might make people angry but I had no idea it would lead to *this*.

CHELLAM. Oh come on, this is the man I glimpsed when you blundered in backstage. I see you, Prab. The *real* you. You know I got to rehearsals early last week. I caught you... *galvanising* the men on the picket line.

PRAB. You're spying on me...?

CHELLAM. It was just so... *compelling*. Like a zombie coming to life. Or... like when the Tin Man finally gets his heart, at the end of that movie. You held their attention, my God, every one of them.

PRAB. Devesh told me to... negotiate with them.

CHELLAM. He told you to ignite the picket line? I don't think so. And then the next day, no picket line.

PRAB *doesn't respond*. CHELLAM *taps his chest*.

I've never met anyone brave enough to stand up to him.

She lets her hand rest there.

PRAB. If he had any sense he'd listen to you.

CHELLAM. Why's that?

PRAB. Because you're smarter than him. Because you're right. You're always right.

CHELLAM. Wow. The words every woman wants to hear...

A moment between them. He backs away. The sound of breaking glass outside.

PRAB. Turn off the lights.

CHELLAM *switches off the lights. They carefully peer out of the window.*

They'll move on. There's nothing to steal.

CHELLAM. I wouldn't want to loot the place – I'd want to destroy it. That poor boy.

Shouting and the sound of breaking glass outside.

PRAB *takes out the blanket and roll-up mattress he's been using as a makeshift bed.*

PRAB. You take this.

He sits on a stool, far away. CHELLAM *bursts into laughter. She rearranges the mattress and blanket into a long seat.*

CHELLAM. Come on. I think I can control myself.

He sits on the mattress. PRAB *idly throws shadow puppets onto the wall in the light of the torch on his phone.* CHELLAM *joins in – she's able to make some shapes he can't.*

PRAB. Is that an elephant?

CHELLAM. Of course.

PRAB. Impressive.

He makes a wolf, roaring at her elephant. She makes the elephant rear up on its hind legs and crush his wolf underfoot.

Hey!

CHELLAM. So, come on. What's the real ending? The version where you haven't got Devesh looking over your shoulder?

PRAB. Do you really want to hear about that?

CHELLAM. Yes! Tell me, I know, it's a huge interspecies orgy.

PRAB. Sure there's an audience for that sort of thing.

CHELLAM. I'm not the writer.

PRAB. That's clear.

CHELLAM. Hey!

They both descend into giggles.

Okay, how about Chandi and the little animals drug
Sengupta and his men, and when they wake up they've been

forced into a re-education programme and all die because
they're soft, bourgeois scum?

PRAB. That's... Okay... Didn't have you down as a Maoist.

CHELLAM. That's it then?

PRAB. I think something like... Chandi rejects Sengupta's offer
and renounces her new status as bullshit. She convinces the
animals to leave for the mountains instead. The future is
unknown, but at least they'll be free to shape it. It's a
struggle at first. There isn't enough food, the valley below is
a wind tunnel and we think they're all going to die.

CHELLAM. But spring comes, and somehow they've made
it... So they start... planting...? Like Sengupta. But not
exactly the same.

PRAB. They focus on biodiversity. Planning. Low-impact
farming.

CHELLAM. They respect the land, and it rewards them.

PRAB. Months pass. A trader comes with supplies for Sengupta
in his new compound, miles away. Before he leaves, the
trader mentions he's on his way to another plantation, in his
former lands. Happy Valley.

CHELLAM. Oh shit.

PRAB. Yep.

CHELLAM. But there's no hierarchy in Happy Valley, right?
No exploitation.

PRAB. They've made the place a community – that's been their
priority. They've built a school, and a medical clinic onsite.

CHELLAM. Run by who?

PRAB. They all do a shift – each of them has something useful
to offer.

CHELLAM. And what about the land? Does it farm itself?

PRAB. They draw up a... rota. They know their shit – they've been doing this their whole lives. They've had to share, and compromise, and collaborate. That's what it's like when you don't have enough, right? But... in Happy Valley, *all* work is recognised – and... valued equally. Planting, weeding, accounting, childcare.

CHELLAM. Fuck, okay.

PRAB. Looking after the elders, cleaning, cooking. They're working for the community, not for profit, so *they* say what things are worth.

CHELLAM. But... I'm a... I dunno, a... lemur monkey. I'm great at planting seeds but I'm not so hot at paperwork. Can't do the... QWERTY keyboard. How do I fit on this rota?

PRAB. All the work is assigned according to their strengths and weaknesses. And... it's recognised some of the work is more repetitive and tedious, so you get time to work the land because it's therapeutic. And some of the work is more physically demanding, so, the more you do of that, the more leisure time you have.

CHELLAM. There is time off, then? In this communist utopia?

PRAB. You're the one giving it a label.

CHELLAM. What would you call it?

PRAB. Sometimes I think the problem is people like the idea but not the... branding.

CHELLAM. Well, yes, there is an image problem.

PRAB. They trade some of their crop when they need things they can't grow themselves. Or, fuck, when they just want stuff – that's fine. They keep a tally of everything, so they only take as much as they need. And... because of that they're able to plan ahead. Store any excess for the winter months. Keep waste to a bare minimum. And... they share stuff. They... don't have to all buy a... ladder, or... a...

CHELLAM. Hoover?

PRAB. Exactly. They have one, or two, and they share them.

CHELLAM. I'm guessing there are a lot of meetings?

They both laugh.

PRAB. Sengupta can't stop thinking about this place, though. He can't accept a young girl showing him up like this.

CHELLAM. Can't we just leave them in peace…? The People's Republic of Talking Animals is a huge success and proves to be an… *inspiration* to mammals around the world.

PRAB. That isn't good story structure.

CHELLAM. It's too easy to tell the sad story.

PRAB. Sengupta and his men travel to the valley and make wild accusations against Chandi. Everything they can think of – theft, abduction, murder.

CHELLAM. So he kills her?

PRAB. Worse than that. He has her arrested on trumped-up charges.

CHELLAM. And of course he's bribed the jury.

PRAB. It's a kangaroo court. Before Chandi even has a chance to speak, the judge is deciding her sentence.

CHELLAM. Which is…?

PRAB. Death. Sorry.

CHELLAM. Arun and the animals won't accept this. They're ready to fight for Happy Valley.

PRAB. That's right.

CHELLAM. Sengupta cannot comprehend that, no matter how many of them he kills, he can never kill an idea.

PRAB. That's good. That would definitely go in.

Beat.

CHELLAM. Shit, I never thought I'd see Devesh taken down like that. And you put me at the centre of it.

Beat.

Things are over with me and him.

PRAB. I thought so.

CHELLAM. I always thought he was different to his dad, deep down... But what happened to that boy, that poor boy. I had to end it.

PRAB. What will you do now?

CHELLAM. Who knows? Mumbai, LA, New York... So many places where people have zero interest in my skills as a jatra performer.

Long beat.

PRAB. You've changed my life.

CHELLAM. If only that was worth something.

Beat.

PRAB. Sounds like it's quietened down out there. I can walk you home.

CHELLAM. There must be an ending where they're just allowed to... live. That's the one you should tell your kid.

CHELLAM *gathers her things together.* PRAB *rolls up the blanket and stuffs it in his bag. They go to leave.* PRAB *takes her arm.*

PRAB. Chellam, there's something I need you to do for me. Something important.

Scene Nineteen

The next morning. PRAB *is in the living room of the duplex in Dum Dum with* KAJOL. *Amba is asleep in her Moses basket.*

KAJOL. Khub Bhalo is in flames.

PRAB. It wasn't me.

KAJOL (*of the window*). You can see the glow, just about. If you really crane your neck. I was scared you got hurt.

PRAB....I didn't know if you'd want me here.

KAJOL. Don't you dare do that. Arsehole. This is your home. This is where you go when the shit hits the fan.

PRAB. Are you okay?

KAJOL. I only know about the riot because Nikhil phoned me. He wasn't sure if you incited it or ran away.

PRAB....Neither.

KAJOL. I thought... I thought maybe you were with her.

PRAB....I was.

KAJOL. Right.

PRAB. I left as soon as it was safe. You know there's nothing between us? You know I would never do that?

KAJOL. I'd like to say yes...

PRAB. It's not who I am.

KAJOL. It's not who you *used* to be.

Beat.

PRAB....I won't walk this tightrope any longer. I've been losing who I am.

KAJOL. What do you mean?

PRAB. The firingi journalist, she gave me a camera. I took pictures of Protham's injuries.

KAJOL. Why?

PRAB. To send to her agency.

KAJOL. And have you?

PRAB *nods*.

Then you have to get it back. Where did you post it from?

PRAB. It's too late.

KAJOL. Will the Nags know it was you?

PRAB.... It could only be me.

KAJOL. Then why would you send it?

PRAB. I did it for Amba.

KAJOL. How is this for Amba? What will they do to us when they find out?

PRAB *hands her an envelope from his pocket. She pulls out a plane ticket.*

There's only one ticket.

PRAB. I had enough to cover the fare for the two of you, for now. I'll join you as soon as I can – before it's published / and Nag finds out.

KAJOL. No. We're not going without you.

PRAB. I'll borrow the money. I have people I can go to.

KAJOL. We don't know anyone with that sort of cash?

PRAB. There are people who'll give what they can. It will add up, I know it will.

KAJOL. How long will that take?

PRAB. We don't have a choice. Right now, we need to get you and Amba as far away as possible.

KAJOL. Khub Bhalo is shut for good – isn't that enough?

PRAB. Nag will just place that big order somewhere else and the same people will turn blind eyes and the same people will get rich. I don't want Amba to grow up in a world where children's limbs are sacrificed to profit.

KAJOL. And I don't want her to grow up in a world without her dad.

PRAB. ... She won't. I promise.

He takes the envelope from her and jots a small map on the back of it.

KAJOL. There must be another way?

PRAB. If I'm wrong, we can come home. If I'm right, and we stay, we'll regret it.

KAJOL *holds him. Amba starts to cry.*

I'll settle her. You pack. I've got someone to meet you at the airport.

KAJOL *exits for the bedroom.* PRAB *sits down beside Amba's Moses basket and gently rocks her. He makes shadow puppets on the wall for her.*

My baba taught me how to do these. The mule... The rabbit... The wolf... The monkey... I don't remember much else about him. He had the day shift while I was at school, and by the time I got home he was getting ready for his other job. Now I wonder when he ever slept...? Ma was the one who taught me things. She taught me everything. And *your* ma is very clever. Much cleverer than me. And I've given you all my stories, now.

He gently lifts Amba from the Moses basket. Kisses her on the forehead and holds her close.

All I want for you, chotto, is for your life to be a gift. Not a trap.

Scene Twenty

Two hours later. CHELLAM *waits in the airport car park.* KAJOL *approaches her, carrying a holdall and wearing Amba in a baby carrier.*

CHELLAM. Where's Prab?

KAJOL. He's not getting this flight. Didn't he tell you?

CHELLAM. No…

KAJOL. I thought you knew.

CHELLAM.…You should go in. Boarding closes soon.

> KAJOL *puts her arm around Amba, as much to comfort herself as the baby.*

When you get to Heathrow, head to the BCP car park. My cousin drives a blue Nissan. Don't worry, I've written it all down.

> *She hands* CHELLAM *a scrap of paper with the information she needs.*

He's skinny and has a salt-and-pepper moustache. I've told him to wear his brown corduroy jacket. If he's with anyone else, or isn't exactly as I've described, don't get in the car. Just hold on to Amba and keep walking.

KAJOL. The Nags don't have people in the UK?

CHELLAM. We don't think so, but you need to keep your wits about you until we're certain. For Amba's sake.

KAJOL. They wouldn't hurt her…?

CHELLAM. They *would*. You have to understand that, okay? You have to let yourself imagine the worst, you must remember the danger you're in to keep yourselves safe.

KAJOL. All I can do is imagine the worst…

CHELLAM. I'm sorry. You'll see him again.

KAJOL. Yes. I know.

CHELLAM. He is a good friend. He became a good friend, I mean.

Beat.

KAJOL. And we were happy. Sometimes.

KAJOL *starts to cry.* CHELLAM *tries to comfort her.*

CHELLAM.... You will be again. One day.

KAJOL. You don't know that.

CHELLAM.... Okay. But right now it's enough to just hide.

CHELLAM *takes an A4 manila envelope out from one of the bags.*

You should have this.

KAJOL. What is it?

CHELLAM. We talked about a new version of the jatra. This is everything I have. You should take it, for Amba.

They go to hug – it's too awkward. CHELLAM *clasps* KAJOL*'s shoulders.*

Good luck.

KAJOL *exits with the bags.*

Scene Twenty-One

The same time. PRAB *is tied to a chair in the back room of Khub Bhalo. He is beaten and bruised. He is trying to free his hands but the cord is too tight.* DEVESH *enters, holding the* Times of India.

DEVESH (*reading from it*). 'As a new report into child labour in the subcontinent is published, we speak to a whistleblower about the life-changing injuries sustained by a child in his workplace.' This is so unfair, my friend. Your big shot at stardom and they don't even print your name.

He holds the paper up.

Little Protham gets a two-page spread, though. His ma will be so excited.

PRAB. She didn't have anything to do with this.

DEVESH. I gave you a job, I gave you a promotion, I gave you a duplex for your sweet little family. I let you fucking write for us. But some firingi journo still wins your loyalty?

PRAB. You don't know anything about loyalty.

DEVESH. Oh I get it. You were doing it for the kids. Fucking 'We Are the World' now, you're bastard Bono, is that it?

PRAB. ...He lost his arm. He almost died.

DEVESH. And he's *still* better off than all the other kids in Hatgachha, because we've covered his medical bills and given his family everything they need.

Beat.

Fuck you, then.

PRAB. Only to keep him quiet.

DEVESH. He's not going to keep quiet, my friend. I've made sure of that. People are already saying how suspicious it is you were here. You weren't supposed to be on shift.

PRAB. You're the one who found him.

DEVESH. Soon, people will be wondering if maybe he got injured because there was some sort of struggle. People will be asking why a young boy would be struggling with a grown man in the back room of a factory.

PRAB. I helped him.

DEVESH. Couple of hundred taka a month to his ma, and his memory will get a bit hazy. Poor kid. That's what trauma does to you.

PRAB. No one will believe that.

DEVESH. People have perverted minds. I blame the media. They'll look back at the money you gave to all those little shits, and they'll think, 'Fuuuuck. He was a serial paedophile. Living here. Right under our noses. But what's the reputation of a dead man worth?

Beat.

You're a smart guy. Smarter than me, definitely. But you still believed I'd make you my right-hand man, without a left-hand man to keep an eye on you. You underestimated your audience, my friend.

Beat.

It's Kajol and Amba I really feel sorry for. Where will they find a priest to bless the ashes of a paedo? It's going to be such a stigma for them. They've left the apartment in a real mess. Had to get the place professionally cleaned. That costs. Clothes everywhere, books on the floor.

PRAB *is disturbed by this but doesn't say anything.*

They didn't take much. Guessing they didn't go far?... Have to admit, my friend, I never recognised this... steely core you have under all that nodding and bowing.

PRAB. Just do what you have to do.

DEVESH. You know I've been reading up, and there isn't a long-lost story about a monkey-fucker called Chandi from the *Mahabharata*.

PRAB. You've got me there.

DEVESH. What happened two years ago?

PRAB. Don't know what you're talking about.

DEVESH. I hear when you were younger you were giving fiery
speeches, leading demonstrations, making people feel
unhappy with their lives. Making people *angry*. I hear some
of your friends disappeared into the forests. Took against
decent business people like my father. But not you. So what
happened?

PRAB *doesn't answer.*

What dampened that fire in your belly?

PRAB. Just get it over with, will you?

DEVESH. That's very practical of you. I'll make sure to let
people know you begged me to end it. Probably out of
shame.

PRAB. I don't care what you say about me.

DEVESH. Nasim's speciality is a razor to the eyeballs. He says
they burst like ripe tomatoes. But I told him not to go there
yet. When Baba was starting up Khub Bhalo, me and Ma were
free labour to him. Every afternoon, I'd run to the workshop
from school, do my share of the overlocking, the seam
unpicking, the cloth-cutting. I was allowed home for dal bhat,
then it was back to the work until bedtime. My teacher called
Ma and Baba to complain I was always tired. Baba wanted to
know one thing – was I one of the smart ones? Could I get
somewhere, really get somewhere, just with my brain? I was
in the middle set for everything – not about to set the world on
fire. The teacher told him I could get into the local college if
I worked hard. Baba said being smart isn't everything. Why
waste his time at the shitty local college when he can start
working on something bigger, right now? And he was right.
I might not be the smartest guy in the room, but I'm the one
who makes everyone shit themselves.

PRAB *leans forward and sniffs.*

PRAB. I don't smell power. I smell... desperation.

DEVESH *swallows his anger. He starts to roughly untie* PRAB*'s wrists, making sure it hurts.*

DEVESH (*of* PRAB*'s injuries*). Do you want to see the sky, one last time?

DEVESH *helps him to his feet.* PRAB *can barely stand.*

Come on, my friend. One last walk under the stars.

They exit.

Epilogue

This evening, the Login Zone in the middle of Leicester city centre. AMBA *rocks her sleeping baby, gazing up at the stars with* PRAB*'s ghost.*

AMBA. Sometimes I enjoy staying out late. I head back in the early hours and the roads are practically empty. Smooth sailing. Gliding. Rolling. *Dreaming.* I pretend someone's on my tail. Makes it more exciting. Keeps my adrenalin up. Sometimes I pretend it's like… a monster. An amorphous, rampaging monster, like… Godzilla, or… The Fog.

PRAB. The Jamie Lee Curtis version or the remake?

AMBA. Either. Or a tsunami I have to outspeed. Or a volcano erupting and I have to go faster or we'll be caught forever in lava and metres of ash like those poor fuckers in Pompei who never saw it coming.

PRAB. There was an increase in earth tremors before the eruption, you know? Vesuvius was still active – it just hadn't exploded for a long time. They knew a cataclysmic event was on the way.

AMBA. Why didn't they leave, then?

PRAB. Complacency? Or… maybe they thought they couldn't change anything so why bother worrying about it?

AMBA. Because they all died.

PRAB. That's pure conjecture, though.

AMBA. Oh I thought they'd told you in person?

PRAB. That's funny.

AMBA. I think so.

PRAB. I saw your big boss online. Californian guy. Seems like a smooth character?

AMBA. If you reach the power-rider list he gives you shares in EatRightNow.

PRAB. Wow.

AMBA. That shit is *worth* something... Not that I'll ever be a fucking power-rider now.

PRAB. But you've got a better idea, chotto.

AMBA. Maybe they're not coming.

PRAB. They will. I can feel it.

AMBA. Is that something they give you? In the afterlife?

PRAB. They don't give you anything.

AMBA. Sounds shit... I should just go home. All I've got is a spare bike light. It's pathetic...

PRAB. No, you've got a question that everyone needs to hear. And you've got an idea of how to answer it.

AMBA. No I haven't.

PRAB. Those words have been running around your head forever. They're on the tip of your tongue.

AMBA. How do you know?

PRAB. Because you're my daughter.

AMBA. I'm not like you.

PRAB. You're better. You're more.

AMBA. You're too much.

Beat.

I used to pretend you were on a trip. Like, for work or something? I used to pretend you'd got held up but you'd be back soon. With presents and stuff. A new sari for Mum.

PRAB. I'd like to buy a new sari for your mum.

AMBA. Someone did a painting of you, you know? A mural. Came up on my Insta feed a few years ago. 'Kolkata Street Art'.

PRAB....Do I have horns? Cloven feet?

AMBA. You look... nice. Whoever did it knew you. Or... I dunno. Had a photo of you or something. I showed Mum. She said they'd caught something about you – the glint in your eye.

PRAB. She said that?

AMBA. She doesn't want to go back, but I'd like to visit one day. See where you used to live. Meet my cousins. Take babs and Kav to see the mural. If we can ever save up enough for the plane fare.

PRAB. Practise on me.

AMBA. What?

PRAB. It's what we used to do. You say it enough times it seems natural. Common sense. Whether you're talking to five people or a hundred.

AMBA....No.

PRAB. Why not?

AMBA. Because it sounds crazy. Childish...

PRAB. Don't say that. Never say that. That's what they want. Come on. My backside's getting wet.

AMBA. How can your arse be... [getting wet, you're a ghost.] Oh for fuck's sake. It's stupid.

PRAB. But getting fired by a billionare over an app isn't?

AMBA. Deactivated.

PRAB. Same thing.

AMBA. It's not that I don't want to be like you. It's more that I'm scared to be.

PRAB. Everyone is scared, chotto. I thought I could do everything by myself, but you know better.

AMBA. Was it worth it…?

PRAB. I couldn't go on pretending the volcano wasn't about to explode.

Beat.

And it was like it was you who'd lost an arm for fifty paisa a day. And then I had no choice.

AMBA. I get it. I do. I just fucking miss you…

AMBA holds her baby closer, overwhelmed. PRAB wants to hold her, but he can't. They remain connected, despite the years, the trauma, and the violence. Three other EATRIGHTNOW RIDERS enter, carrying their delivery bags, cycle helmets, motorcycle helmets. They can't see PRAB because he's dead.

(*To herself.*) Fuck.

They hug and fist-bump their hellos, the baby is cooed over.

EATRIGHTNOW RIDER 1. Alright? Haven't been waiting long, have you?

AMBA. Me? No, I was early.

EATRIGHTNOW RIDER 2 (*of the baby*). Oh my God, he gets cuter every time I see him!

EATRIGHTNOW RIDER 1 (*starting to unpack food from their delivery box*). Mo sneaked a load of spicy wedges through for us.

EATRIGHTNOW RIDER 2. Legend.

EATRIGHTNOW RIDER 1. And he put a fiver towards Grant's bike.

EATRIGHTNOW RIDER 3. I can too.

EATRIDENOW RIDER 3 puts some money in an envelope that EATRIGHTNOW RIDER 1 holds out.

EATRIGHTNOW RIDER 2. Nice.

AMBA glances at PRAB, *uncertain. Beat.*

AMBA. I've been thinking… if there's a load of us coming down tonight, it would be good to talk about our pay?

EATRIGHTNOW RIDER 1. You mean how shit it is?

AMBA. Yeah. Pretty much…

AMBA speaks to them all, one eye on PRAB.

Like, I heard EatRightNow can afford to pay riders in Newcastle six quid per hour and two quid per drop. So how come we only get piece rates?

EATRIGHTNOW RIDER 1. They get paid per hour?

EATRIGHTNOW RIDER 3. Didn't you know?

EATRIGHTNOW RIDER 2. Thought that had been phased out.

EATRIGHTNOW RIDER 1. What are we supposed to do about it?

AMBA. We're already doing it, sort of. Helping Grant out, and Ruby.

EATRIGHTNOW RIDER 1. How'd you mean?

AMBA. We're supposed to look at Grant and be happy he lost his bike, right? One less rider to compete with.

EATRIGHTNOW RIDER 3. Bit harsh.

EATRIGHTNOW RIDER 2. You know what she means though.

AMBA. They're always trying to do that. Make us run off in different directions to try to catch a single hare. Because they know. If we work together we might bring down the stag.

EATRIGHTNOW RIDER 3. The stag?

AMBA.…We can't take a sick day if we're sick…

She's nervous, but is spurred on by PRAB.

We can't take maternity leave if we're pregnant. We won't get a pension. We're never going to be able to own our own place, do anything but flatshare. But the thing is, the reason we don't have sick pay, or holiday pay, or maternity pay, is because they pretend we're not staff. Pretend they're not our bosses.

EATRIGHTNOW RIDER 2. I get to tell my mum I'm an entrepreneur, though.

AMBA. EatRightNow don't want to hear from us if something goes wrong, or something's fucked up at work. But if they pretend they're not our bosses, it means we don't have to tell them if we're going to strike.

EATRIGHTNOW RIDER 1. Strike?

EATRIGHTNOW RIDER 2. For what?

EATRIGHTNOW RIDER 3. Six quid per hour sounds pretty good to me.

EATRIGHTNOW RIDER 1. It'd be a start.

AMBA. I know, right?

EATRIGHTNOW RIDER 3. What else?

AMBA. We can work it out together. (*Looking to* PRAB.) Start putting down our ideas now. It's not up to me. It's up to *us*.

AMBA *and the other* EATRIGHTNOW RIDERS *sit together and discuss their demands, noting them down on their phones. The baby is passed around, cuddled and coddled. They demolish the wedges. Share a joke. Listen to one another. Slow fade to blackout.*

Ends.

SONALI BHATTACHARYYA

Sonali Bhattacharyya is an award-winning playwright and screenwriter (Sonia Friedman Production Award and Theatre Uncut Political Playwriting Award for *Chasing Hares*).

Her plays include *Two Billion Beats* (Orange Tree Theatre), *Megaball* (National Theatre Learning), *Slummers* (Cardboard Citizens/Bunker Theatre), *The Invisible Boy* (Kiln Theatre) and *2066* (Almeida Theatre).

Sonali is a graduate of the Royal Court Writers' Group, the Old Vic 12, and Donmar Warehouse's Future Forms Programme and recipient of the Bertha Foundation Artivism Award. She is currently under commission to Fifth Word, Kiln Theatre, Tara Arts and Donmar Warehouse, and is developing a drama series for television with Dancing Ledge Productions and an Augmented Reality project with Anagram.

www.sonaliwrites.com

A Nick Hern Book

Chasing Hares first published in Great Britain in 2022 as a paperback original by Nick Hern Books Limited, The Glasshouse, 49a Goldhawk Road, London W12 8QP, in association with the Young Vic, London, and Theatre Uncut

Chasing Hares copyright © 2022 Sonali Bhattacharyya

Sonali Bhattacharyya has asserted her right to be identified as the author of this work

Cover Artwork: Art direction by Emilie Chen. Photography by Rosaline Shahnavaz.

Designed and typeset by Nick Hern Books, London
Printed in Great Britain by Mimeo Ltd, Huntingdon, Cambridgeshire PE29 6XX

A CIP catalogue record for this book is available from the British Library

ISBN 978 1 83904 101 3

Woodland CARBON
www.woodlandcarbon.co.uk
NICK HERN BOOKS
Printed on Carbon Captured paper